THE POWER TO SOAR HIGHER

THE POWER TO SOAR HIGHER

Peter Legge
with
Tashon Ziara

Eaglet Publishing

Eaglet Publishing
Peter Legge Management Co. Ltd.
4th Floor, 4180 Lougheed Highway
Burnaby, British Columbia, V5C 6A7, Canada
Tel. (604) 299-7311 Fax (604) 299-9188

Library and Archives Canada Cataloguing in Publication

Legge, Peter, 1942-
    The power to soar higher / by Peter Legge with Tashon Ziara.

ISBN 978-0-9781459-5-8

1. Success. 2. Self-actualization (Psychology). I. Ziara, Tashon
    II. Title.

BF637.S8L45358 2008   158.1   C2008-905832-1

Third Printing

Jacket design by Catherine Mullaly; cover photo Dina Goldstein; electronic imaging by Debbie Craig; Typeset by Ina Bowerbank
Edited by Kim Mah
Printed and bound in Canada by Transcontinental

Dedicated to
my first grandson

Benjamin David
(Born August 14, 2006)

and to
my wife Kay
on our 40th wedding anniversary

"A wedding anniversary is the celebration of love, trust,
partnership, tolerance and tenacity.
The order varies for any given year."
— Paul Sweeney

Other Books by the Author

How to Soar With the Eagles
You Can If You Believe You Can
It Begins With a Dream
If Only I'd Said That
If Only I'd Said That: Volume II
If Only I'd Said That: Volume III
If Only I'd Said That: Volume IV
Who Dares Wins
The Runway of Life
Make Your Life a Masterpiece
The Power of Tact

Booklets

97 Tips on How to Do Business in Tough Times
97 Tips on Customer Service
97 Tips on How to Jumpstart Your Career

CD

The Runway of Life

ACKNOWLEDGEMENTS

This is the 12th book that I've published in the past 15 years. I want to thank the thousands of readers who have helped make all of them Canadian bestsellers.

Thank you also for the encouragement to keep on writing and sharing my life with you in simple and easy-to-understand concepts, principles and stories.

This book, *The Power to Soar Higher: How to Build a Gold Medal Business*, is a collection of principles that have had an influence on my life and my business, and I believe they have all been for the good.

I am also thankful for my own gold medal team, who have come together to create and publish this book. Teams are so important to the success of any venture and to paraphrase Jim Collins from his book *From Good to Great*, "get the right people on the bus, in the right seats, all going the same way and miracles can happen."

I'm grateful that I got the right people on my bus, and would like to take this opportunity to acknowledge their efforts:

Kim Mah — Our keen-eyed editor can always be counted on to ensure my words are as clear and polished as can be.

Cathy Mullaly — Our talented art director. Whether she's designing the latest issue of our award-winning *BCBusiness* magazine, or putting together this dust jacket, her creativity never ceases to amaze me.

Ina Bowerbank — Our hardworking typographer. Her meticulous eye for detail is unsurpassed in the business.

Corinne Smith — The Vice President, Production, at Canada Wide Media is a stickler for keeping all our projects on time and on budget, and this book would not be possible without her management skills.

Dale Clarke — Where would I be without my remarkable personal assistant? With her positive attitude and enthusiasm, she keeps me well organized and prepared no matter how many commitments I'm juggling each day.

Tashon Ziara — My unparalleled writer, editor and researcher. Her unique passion for words has brought my stories and ideas to life in ways I could not have imagined.

I hope you enjoy the read as much as I enjoyed the journey.

Peter Legge, O.B.C.

TABLE OF CONTENTS

Making an Impact:

Attitude is Everything:

Service Matters:

Building Relationships:

Opportunity Knocks:

Never Stop Learning:

Living With Gratitude:

INTRODUCTION

All our lives, we are learning from others, whether we're learning how to be more effective in our work, how to get along better with our clients and colleagues or how to follow our dreams. The multi-talented and accomplished Renaissance man Michelangelo was reported to have said, "And yet I am still learning."

Charlie "Tremendous" Jones, one of my Speakers Roundtable associates, has a famous line used around the world: "We will be the same person we are today in five years, except for the people we meet, the places we go and the books we read."

I've been running my company Canada Wide Media for 33 years now without losing money in even one single year, I have been successfully married to the same woman for nearly 40 years as of this writing and I continue to work on my integrity and reputation in the community through my interactions with others every day.

My life is a reflection of all of the things I have learned through-out the years from the people I've met, the numerous places I've had the good fortune to visit, the thousands of books I've read and the community organizations that I've become involved in . . . and yet I am still learning. In fact, here are five things that I've learned just in the last six months:

Firstly, in looking to hire someone to work for your company, you need to find a person with the following three qualities:

a. Integrity
b. Intelligence
c. Energy

The most important of these is integrity, because if they don't have integrity, the other two qualities — intelligence and energy — are going to kill you. All success begins with integrity.

Second, here's an exercise that my friend Brian Tracy does with audiences in his seminars:

Take 30 seconds and write down your three most important priorities in life (by the way, Brian points out that 30 seconds is as accurate as 30 minutes because it forces you to go with your gut reaction).

1. _____
2. _____
3. _____

Now, look at what you've highlighted. Ninety per cent of people will have written down some version of the following:

1. Relationships/family
2. Financial/wealth
3. Health/well being

Now ask yourself, "How do I achieve these objectives?"

The third pearl of wisdom comes from Vancouver businessman Bob Lee.

"Always tell the truth, always be honest and in the long haul you will do all the right things. Make money — yes. But more importantly, take the time to learn how to invest and handle money."

W. Clement Stone once said, "If you cannot save money, then the seeds of greatness are not in you."

My fourth point comes courtesy of golf legend Jack Nicklaus:

My company produced the Telus Skins official program for the 2006 golf tournament that was held at Nicklaus North golf course in Whistler, B.C. During the tournament, my wife Kay and I had the opportunity to walk in the crowd that was following the legendary all-time PGA champion Jack Nicklaus.

As he prepared to take his second shot on the 12th hole, Nicklaus turned to his caddie and asked, "How far is the green?" Glancing down the fairway, his caddie responded, "About 91 or 92 yards." Jack quickly turned to him and said, "Well, which is it — 91 or 92 yards?"

Talk about precision.

Thinking about it later I realized that while it wouldn't make that much difference to you or me if we judged the distance to the pin that precisely, Jack's entire career as a champion was built on his ability to get that ball as close to the pin as possible. In his world, one yard could be the difference between sinking that all-important putt to win the tournament or having to take another stroke and end up being out of the money.

The fifth point that I want to share with you is about commitment:

My wife Kay and I celebrate our 40th wedding anniversary on November 23, 2008. I often say, "I'm not the lover I once was, but I'm more in love than I once was."

Whether it is in the pursuit of life goals, building a business, working in the community or in their marriages and relationships with others, many people want to take shortcuts. But life has a way of rewarding those who work hard. If you spend a little more time and hours on your craft, you will find hard work is much like compound interest in your bank account; it almost grows by itself.

I've found that all of life is much like that. When Kay and I are asked how we have managed to stay together for 40 years we both say the same thing, "We have worked hard at it!"

That's life, business, speaking, building financial independence, relationships, family and marriage . . . if you truly want to Soar Higher, you have to make a commitment to work at it and invest yourself for the long haul.

That being said, what are you doing today to become the person you want to be?

This book is full of the wisdom that I have gathered from others over a lifetime of learning and I have deliberately kept the chapters short to make it an easy reference so that you can come back to it time and again.

All the best to you as you continue on your journey.

Peter Legge

IT BEGINS WITH A DREAM

1

DREAM BIG DREAMS

If we're lucky, each of us will live for about 4,420 weeks. When you think about how quickly a week goes by, it seems like a lot less than 85 years. Therefore, my advice is if you're planning to live life to the fullest and have the opportunity to explore all of those inviting corners, you have to hustle. You have to dream big dreams and *live them.*

It takes a bit of courage to live your dreams, but I know you've got what it takes and you do too! If you don't believe me, just think of all the times you have discovered that you actually *can* achieve what you set out to do. Yet, remember how nervous you were going into that seemingly impossible challenge? The halting steps. But you did it, you believed in yourself and you went ahead anyway. Afterwards, did you say to yourself, "Hey, that wasn't so difficult, what's next?" Or did you settle back into your comfortable niche once again and praise yourself for the next 250 weeks?

Every millionaire or billionaire I've ever talked to tells me that the biggest secret to his or her success has been to dream big dreams, plan for the long term and keep moving forward. These people didn't get where they are by taking a leisurely bus ride up the hill, they decided early on that they were going to the very top of the mountain and they began to chart a course that would get them there.

Microsoft billionaire Bill Gates, a man whom we all watch and listen to with great interest, says that his success in business has largely been the result of his ability to focus on long-term goals and ignore short-term distractions. Despite all of his success, he continues to dream big dreams about developments within his own industry and he creates the opportunities — bringing together the right people and the right technology — that can make them happen.

"When change is inevitable," says Mr. Gates, "you must spot it, embrace it and find ways to make it work for you." That's first-hand advice from someone who dreams big dreams and has literally changed the world as a result.

Of course, it can be intimidating to compare our own lives to that of someone like Bill Gates. You might say to yourself that he was the right person in the right place at the right time; that he got the breaks; or that no one will ever again succeed quite like he has succeeded. When comparing bank accounts that may well be. But while Mr. Gates may have a special niche in the business world, there is also a special niche in the world for you — you just have to find it.

When I talk of dreaming, I'm not talking about daydreaming. Dreaming also involves doing. You dream your big dream and you start to make it come true. You write it down and share it with your spouse or a close friend. You begin to plot your course and look for likeminded people who can help you along the way, you breathe some life into it, keep fanning the flames that will make it burn brighter and remember that everything that you do, say or think counts.

I myself have dreamed big dreams and many of them have come true as a result. And I keep dreaming, reaching out a little more, taking calculated risks, believing that if I've climbed this far — and the view has been fantastic — then I can certainly continue to climb higher and higher.

We humans thrive on achievement and the bigger we dream, the more we can achieve. Vancouver billionaire Jimmy Pattison once told me that those men and women who dare to dream big dreams are the only ones who will achieve big dreams.

A case in point: Canadian Jim Carrey was a stand-up comic playing the comedy club circuit in North America who dreamed of international stardom. Following his acclaimed success in the movies *Ace Ventura: Pet Detective*, *The Mask* and *Batman Forever*, he was interviewed on a Barbara Walters television special. In the interview, he talked about his struggle to make it at the beginning of his career, the long, lonely nights on the road and how six or seven years previously he had written a cheque to himself for $10 million and dated it October 1995. He kept this huge dream in his wallet, looking at it every day. In 1995, Jim Carrey signed a contract to star in the sequel to *Ace Ventura* for — you guessed it — $10 million. Shortly afterward, he received a record sum for a comedy actor when he was paid $20 million to star in the movie *The Cable Guy*. Today, Carrey continues to dream big dreams and continually reinvent himself as an actor by exploring new territory.

Was it coincidence, fate or luck that Carrey was able to realize his big dream — or the fact that he carried his dream around with him every single day to keep him focused and moving towards his goal?

"You become what you think about most of the time." It's a thought that has been attributed to many people, but I remember it coming from the late, great motivator Earl Nightingale. It's a truth than never loses its resonance.

Ralph Waldo Emerson, who spoke and wrote with eloquence about almost everything, said, "If the single man plant himself indomitably on his instincts, and there abide, the huge world will come round to him." I interpret that to mean that while it may take time and while we may have to struggle to find what we're looking for, if we stay focused on what we want to achieve, it will come to fruition.

Of course, in any hunt for treasure, it helps to have a map, the keys to secret doors and the password to enter the hidden chamber . . . you can begin right now with Secret No. 1 (which, as I say elsewhere in this book isn't really a secret): Identify your big dream. Dream it. Do it.

We humans thrive on achievement and the bigger we dream, the more we can achieve.

2

ARE YOU A PRISONER
TO YOUR POTENTIAL?

Last summer, my wife Kay and I had a unique opportunity to cruise the Mediterranean on a small cruise ship called *The Seaborn Legend* from Monte Carlo to Nice. There were only 196 passengers, which made for an intimate and relaxing voyage.

At one of the ports of call along the way we took a day trip to see the city of Florence. Our first tourist visit of the day was to the museum Galleria dell'Accademia where we got a first-hand look at the 13-and-a-half-foot sculpture of David by Michelangelo. It took him three years to finish this colossus.

As you walk slowly towards "The David" you are reminded that Michelangelo worked on 45 sculptures in his lifetime and only completed 14 of them (if each completed work took three years, that would be 42 years of work). David and Moses are probably the most famous of those that he did complete. As you approach "The David" you pass by unfinished statues called *The Prisoners, Atlantis, The Young Slave, The Beardless Slave* and *The Awakening Slave*. These are the unfinished works and unfulfilled potential of a true genius.

It's been said by some people that the average person generally develops only about two per cent of his or her potential over a lifetime, although others estimate that we use as much as 10 per cent of our potential. I imagine if you were to use 25 per cent of your potential, you would be called a genius like Michelangelo.

Given these estimates, what's truly astonishing is the amount of potential we will never use. Even if we double the higher number of 10 per cent to 20 per cent, that still leaves five per cent of our potential untapped. Wow! What an opportunity we all have to better ourselves.

The best part is that it doesn't take much to start using more of our potential. As we look around our workplace, our community and even our home life, we can clearly see our own "blocks of stone" that, as yet, have not been developed in order to unlock our hidden potential.

How best to start?

Associate yourself with mentors and other motivated people who will help you stretch your potential and reach new heights. Like Michelangelo, who chose to extend his reach as far as possible, you may not be able to finish everything you start, but somewhere in the midst of all that you endeavour to do, you might just find your own masterpiece. So get out those tools and start chipping away at your own sculpture to maximize your life, make the most of your abilities and uncover your true potential.

You may not be able to finish everything you start, but somewhere in the midst of all that you endeavour to do, you might just find your own masterpiece.

3

WRITE IT DOWN, MAKE IT HAPPEN

In one way or another, most of us keep some kind of a record of the things we have to do. Almost everywhere around you, whether you're in a business meeting, riding in the office elevator or taking the commuter train home, you'll see people pulling out their BlackBerries, daytimers or scraps of paper to record all kinds of things: what they believe is important information gleaned from a presentation, the date and time of upcoming business and social events, a reminder to get the oil changed in their car.

Technology has made all of this recordkeeping a lot easier for us. With all of our devices synched, we can transfer data at the touch of a button to help us keep track of our lives and remind us about what we have to do today, tomorrow and weeks, months or even years into the future.

Interestingly, the more we use these devices, the more dependent we become upon them. It's like having an external memory that we can download to so we don't have to carry everything around in our heads. I can tell you, the older you get and the more you have to remember, the more you appreciate these devices, especially when you can't remember something like where you parked the car. Even if we haven't done it ourselves, we've all seen people wandering around parking lots or up and down between the levels of the parkade trying to remember, was it 3B or 4B? The next time, they will most likely make a note of where they parked the car and won't have to wander around, looking lost.

There's nothing wrong or unusual about writing down important things that you want to remember. In fact, it's on my list of secrets that aren't really secrets at all and it works just as well for goals as it does for remembering where you parked your car.

You wouldn't think that you'd forget what your goals are just because you didn't write them down, but often that's exactly what happens. When you actually have a goal written down and placed in a strategic location, you automatically increase the number of times that you think about your goal. A friend of mine told me that five years from now she and her husband will own a bed and breakfast/cooking school in the south of France. She wrote that promise to herself on a piece of paper and stuck it to her refrigerator with a magnet. I have no doubt that five years from now, the planned business will be open and thriving. It will happen because she wants it to happen and every day she is reminded of her goal.

Sometimes I think we neglect to write things down because we don't believe we'll really end up doing what we *say* we'll be ... This is a mistake if we truly want to achieve our goals ... putting it down on paper can jumpstart our ... down makes it clear, tangible and ... get our mind work- ... sciously. Writing ... ps we can take to

... te down? Well, you ... lottery, but, while ... something you can ... lude both short- and long-term goals that can be reached if you put your heart, mind and energy behind what you're planning to do. They can be a mixture of things that involve your career and your family. More often than not, the two are inseparable anyway.

A good place to start is by thinking about what you *expect* to be doing a year from now and what you would *like* to be doing a year from now. Would you like to own a bed and breakfast in the south of France? If that's your goal and you believe it's attainable, write it down and add the subheads that go with it, such as:

- get brochures of existing B&Bs in the region,
- check out the competition,
- research regulations,
- take French lessons,
- find out if the kids can go to school in France,
- contact the French consulate for residency information,
- talk to various B&B owners to find out more about the business, etc.

As you complete the various items on your list, not only will you get a clearer picture of what it will take to realize your goal, but you will also be able to determine whether or not you are willing to go the distance and really make it happen.

Complete this planning process for each goal on your "plate of possibilities" and pretty soon you will have a much clearer picture of where you want to go with your life. For instance, if your career isn't exactly matching your talents and you think it may be time for a change, why not make a *time* investment in things you like to do to find out if another career might suit you better. For example, if you love photography and you think you could make a go of it as a professional, maybe it's time to take some evening classes that will take you from being merely good to being consistently excellent. Write it down and check it out.

Alternatively, perhaps you don't mind the company you're working for but would rather work in the office in Seattle. Could you make a move? Write it down and check it out.

Although there's no right or wrong way to manage your goals, it might help to put them into groups that cover off such things as job, financial, kids, spouse, etc. Be as specific as you can with each goal. If you want to keep it a secret, that's up to you, but others may be interested in knowing where you're hoping to go and, who knows, they may even be able to help you along the way. However you organize it, the real goal is to discover what you want to accomplish, develop a clear sense of direction and then GET MOVING ON IT (that's another of my not-so-secret secrets of success).

Writing down your goals doesn't just help you remember them; it can also be a useful tool in helping you to develop a clear sense of direction.

4

JUST DO IT

"It takes as much energy to wish
as it does to plan."
— Eleanor Roosevelt

As far as I'm concerned, the Nike slogan "Just Do It" has got to be one of the simplest and most effective advertising slogans ever invented. It's also the best piece of advice that I would give to anyone who has a goal that they want to accomplish.

When I look at my own life and my career, I can honestly say that it is the times when I acted on my own initiative and just did it, which I am most proud of. Like when I first met Kay while I was working as an emcee on a cruise ship. If I hadn't grabbed the opportunity, when that cruise was over, Kay would have sailed out of my life forever. Instead, this year we will be celebrating our 40th wedding anniversary.

Likewise, when I first came upon the idea that I should write a book to elaborate on the topics that I present in my speeches and expand my audience. If I had waited to get a publisher, I might still be waiting to publish my first book. Instead, because I decided to get it out there and publish it myself, today you are reading my 12th book.

"Just do it" is a reminder for us to get going, to stop procrastinating and fretting over whatever roadblocks our mind is throwing up to hold us back. It's a reminder to focus on the present moment — the task at hand — and forget about the rest (at least for a while).

Getting started is often the most difficult part of any new undertaking. It's kind of like learning to drive a car with a manual transmission; the first gear is the hardest to master, but once you've figured out when to let out the clutch and you start to move forward, shifting into the next gear is suddenly much easier.

Here are some ideas to help you "Just do it!" in your own life:

Set concrete, attainable goals and act on them.
"I'm going to update my resume and send it to 10 companies that I would love to work for" is more likely to succeed than, "I'm going to get my act together." Be specific about what you want to achieve and then get going.

Commit to your plan.
Tell others about your plan and use your network to get things moving. It's much harder to back down when others know what you are doing. For example, in 2004, when I heard that the Innovation Centre in my local community of Coquitlam, B.C., wanted to provide a library of business and motivational books for visitors, I immediately committed to providing them with 1,000 books to get the collection started. My next step was to let my network of fellow speakers and business leaders know about my plan. Before I knew it, I had collected literally thousands of great books to help people learn about topics such as goal setting, entrepreneurship and leadership. I was absolutely

thrilled when I found out that they were going to call the facility the Peter Legge Library.

Believe in yourself and be willing to take a few risks.
When I set out to publish my first book I didn't know if anyone would actually buy it and I worried about what I would do with a roomful of books if they didn't. In the end, I decided that it was better to find out for sure (even if I failed) rather than live my life wondering, "What if I had taken the chance?"

"Action may not always bring happiness, but there is no happiness without action."
— Benjamin Disraeli

5

NO ONE DREAMS OF MAKING IT SMALL

While on a trip to New York I was reading *New York Magazine*, when I spotted an ad that I believe was for either an insurance company or an investment firm and it caught my attention. It simply said, "No one dreams of making it small."

My Speakers Roundtable colleague Nido Qubein says if you are going to think, think big.

That's really what this book, *The Power to Soar Higher*, is all about. Each one of us has a limited amount of time to gather the resources and master the skills that will help us to make it big.

In 1991, I had the unique pleasure of being on the same program as Og Mandino for a sold-out engagement at Vancouver's Orpheum Theatre. You could say I was his warm-up act. One of the things he said that has stuck with me is, "I am here for a purpose and that purpose is to grow into a mountain, not to shrink to a grain of sand. Henceforth, I will apply all my efforts to become the highest mountain of all and I will strain my potential until it cries for mercy."

If you know your talents and develop them passionately, you will understand what the real power of Soaring Higher is all about.

When I bought my first magazine *TV Week* more than 30 years ago, I did it with the intention of making it big and I invested everything I had into it, which included mortgaging my house. I took a chance and risked it all. If I succeeded — as I had every intention of doing — the money I borrowed would be repaid out of the profits of the company in the first five years of operation. If I failed, I would lose my business and my home. I couldn't fail.

As determined as I was to succeed, my competition didn't take me seriously. At the time, the *TV Guide* head office was run out of Toronto and for the first five to 10 years that I was in business, the head guy in Toronto would regularly call the Vancouver office and ask, "How long will this guy be around?" And each time they would tell him, "Don't worry, it won't be long now." He kept calling and asking and 30 years later, they ended up going out of business and we bought their local operation.

Before we went ahead with the *TV Guide* acquisition, I carefully worked through the numbers and then I called my longtime mentor Joe Segal, who listened to what I had to say and then told me that as far as he was concerned, the only thing I needed to do was write the cheque for $250,000.

He was right.

No matter how big you get
or how secure your market appears to be,
never underestimate your competition.
Chances are they're hungrier than you.

Think for yourself and do your homework,
then seek the advice of your mentors
before acting. They will either validate the
decision you have already made or
point out serious oversights that could cost
you dearly. Either way, you win.

6

IT'S NEVER TOO LATE
TO PURSUE YOUR DREAM

When my wife Kay and I were first married, we didn't have a lot of money; nevertheless, we agreed that Kay would be an at-home mother for our children. As a result, she spent the first 15 years of our marriage attending to the needs of our three daughters, Samantha, Rebecca and Amanda. It was an investment of her time that pays wonderful dividends today in that we have three spectacular and accomplished daughters, each of whom is pursuing her own dreams.

Kay had a dream too. Even before she had children, Kay dreamed of becoming a marriage counsellor and helping others. That dream didn't change throughout the years that Kay was nurturing our daughters — if anything, it became stronger. So it was that as the girls matured into young women and didn't need Kay nearly so much, her thoughts returned once again to pursuing her dream.

Realizing that she would need to return to university to complete both a BA and a Masters degree to realize her goal, Kay worried that she had left it too long. "It's going to take almost six years and I'll be nearly 50 by the time I graduate," she said to me one evening.

"Whether you do it or not, in six years you will be 50 anyway," I responded. "So why not go for it?"

Kay decided to follow her heart and she did it. After completing her BA, Kay enrolled in the Masters of Counselling program at Trinity Western University and today she works two days a week at a clinic in Langley, B.C. She's been doing it for 10 or 11 years now and she absolutely loves it. Her mission, she says, is to try to get people to come together and there is no doubt in my mind that by having the courage to pursue her own dream, she has enriched the lives of others and made the world a better place.

If you have a dream of any kind, it's never too late to go out and do it. Why not get started right now?

7

BACK TO CAPISTRANO

On several occasions I have driven down Interstate 5 in Southern California and every time I do, as I get close to San Juan Capistrano I can't help but think about the swallows. I've never been there on March 19, St. Joseph's Day, but this is the date every year when the residents of Capistrano celebrate the return of the swallows from their winter home in Argentina. Every year, just like clockwork, huge clouds of swallows descend to spend the summer months in and around the old Mission, which is protected as a bird sanctuary.

For those of us who fly the international air routes with any regularity and appreciate the great distances, the migratory achievements of birds seem all the more miraculous as we gaze from the windows of aircraft than they do when we simply read about them. It's almost unfathomable that they can travel such distances.

The story of the journey of the Capistrano swallows is as fascinating as any in the world of our feathered friends when you consider that in any given year, each of these small birds will fly 12,000 miles roundtrip from Argentina to California and back again. Most of those miles are over water. That's a lot of flapping!

Unlike a 747, swallows can't make the entire trip between their summer and winter homes without a break. So how do they manage? While it sounds incredible, I've been told that each swallow carries with it in its beak a small twig. When the bird gets tired, the twig becomes the "boat" on which it rests while bobbing about on the water until it is ready to continue on its journey.

Now, I have no idea whether this is completely true or simply a legend that has been passed down through the years, but I like to believe it for the simple reason that it is an inspiring thought and any time anyone or anything has a dream or a goal of such great dimension, it gives me the motivation to achieve my own goals and pursue my own dreams. Of course, twig or no twig, the fact that these birds are committed to make the journey year after year is truly amazing. We can learn a lot about courage and stamina from these little swallows that know exactly where they are going and are willing to give everything they've got to get there.

Is there something in your
own life that you have been trying to
build up the courage to do?
Take a cue from the swallows of Capistrano
and begin your journey today.

8

WHAT'S YOUR OLYMPIC DREAM?

Mark Twain once said, "Twenty years from now you will be more disappointed by the things you didn't do than by the ones you did. So throw off the bowlines. Sail away from the safe harbour. Catch the trade winds in your sails. Explore. Dream. Discover."

It's blessedly true that any embarrassment we may feel as a result of past mistakes eventually fades with the passage of time as we learn to forgive and — if we're really smart — even laugh at our own foibles. But somehow, it's not the same with the shoulda, coulda, woulda's. For some reason, they tend to only get stronger as the years go by. That's why I have resolved in my own life to chase as many of my dreams as I possibly can, even my Olympic dream.

"Peter has an Olympic dream!" you say to yourself with just a hint of surprise upon reading this . . . "Isn't he, like, over 60 years old?"

It's true, I am over 60, so luckily for me, my Olympic dream doesn't involve a ski ramp, a world pole-vaulting record or a spot on the Jamaican bobsled team. My Olympic dream is to be emcee of the opening ceremonies at the Vancouver 2010 Winter Olympic Games. The idea came to me after John Furlong, CEO of the Vancouver Organizing Committee for the Olympics, asked me and 17 other individuals to be 2010 Winter Olympic and Paralympic Games ambassadors.

In creating the Ambassador Program, John's mission was to touch the soul of the nation and inspire the world by creating and delivering an extraordinary Olympic and Paralympic experience. At the breakfast where the first 18 ambassadors met, he presented each of us with a unique gold Olympic pin that would be ours alone. He then asked everyone what their Olympic dream was. When my turn came, I said that my Olympic dream was to be the English-speaking master of ceremonies for the Opening Ceremonies at the 2010 Olympics. Talk about your Olympic-sized dream, but John himself has always said, "Dream big!"

In the few years since the Ambassador Program started, most of the people that I have worked with at the Olympics, including Rick Turner (the government liaison for the 2010 Games), have all known about my dream. At the beginning, however, it wasn't taken quite as seriously as I'd intended. But as time passed and I continued to talk about it, most everyone has realized that I was, and am, dead serious. As a result, about six months ago I got an email from Rick Turner that asked, "Are you bilingual or could you be bilingual?" With that simple question, suddenly I was filled with hope, so I started to reply that although I was not, if I knew now with still two years to go, I could go to France and study or do whatever else I needed to do to keep the door of opportunity open.

Then, just before I pressed send, I had another thought, "Who do I know that is bilingual, female (to offset my masculine charm, of course), and would be willing to do this with me so that I could convince the Olympic people to give me a shot?" The thought that popped into my head almost immediately is that my middle daughter Rebecca is fluently bilingual. So I changed my proposal to this, "How about the first father and daughter, English and French co-emcees of the Opening Ceremonies for the Olympics?" I pressed send and off it went.

Now I was sitting there thinking to myself, anybody could do that. Anybody could send an email. I've got to do something different . . . and spectacular, just like the Olympics. So I sat there, staring out my window, wondering, "What can I do that is different and special?"

An hour passed, then two hours, then three . . . finally, it came to me: go and rent a TV studio, hire the best cameraman in the city, find a great producer, hire the best makeup artist, borrow some Olympic footage from John Furlong and produce your own mock Opening Ceremonies.

So that's exactly what I did. I spent $15,000 to put together a 10-minute DVD (for a job that doesn't pay anything) and both Rick Turner and John Furlong, along with David Atkins (the producer of the Opening Ceremonies), were suitably impressed.

As of this writing, I don't have the job and I might not get the job, but I have to say it gives me a thrill just to watch that video and know that I went all out to pursue my Olympic dream. For the last 50 speeches that I have given, I have also used this story and the video to close my presentation. And at the very end of each presentation, I ask the audience, "What is your Olympic dream? And what are you prepared to do, how far are you prepared to go, to make that dream a reality? Is it to have a great marriage, to have a wonderful relationship with your children, to be known as someone who brings integrity and honesty to all of their business dealings? Whatever your dream is, now is the time to get started."

———————————

Some you win, some you lose
and some get rained out . . . I'm going
to give it my very, very best
at all times and in the end, be content
in the knowledge that when it
was my time to shine, I went for the gold!

———————————

"SECRETS OF SUCCESS"

9

NO SECRETS — OR SHORTCUTS — TO SUCCESS

Last year, I was asked to speak at the University of British Columbia's Sauder School of Business to a group of second- and third-year students studying in the Bachelor of Commerce program. During the reception prior to my speech, I chatted with many of the students and asked them what exactly they wanted me to talk about in my address.

"We want to know the secrets of success," they told me. They also asked me to tell them if, in my opinion, there were any shortcuts to achieving success.

By the time I took the podium, I knew what I wanted to say. The greatest secret to being successful in life, whether it be in business, as a spouse or parent, an athlete or inventor, a philanthropist or a friend, I told them, is that there are no secrets. You have to follow your heart and do what you know to be right for you. There are as many ways to define success as there are people on this planet and what works for one person is not guaranteed to work for another.

I touched on this in the very first book I wrote, titled *It Begins With a Dream,* in which I spoke about the two most important things that you can do to guarantee success in life — keep in mind the only reason that anyone would think these are secrets is because so many people ignore the advice. The first is to "Dream Big Dreams," and the second is to "Do What You Love To Do!"

I added the exclamation mark because this is advice that needs to be shouted so everyone can hear.

Too many times I meet people who are bored, unhappy, dissatisfied, frustrated or angry that the job they have isn't the one they truly want. Yet they stick it out year after year.

Why?

Is it fear of failure?

Laziness?

Lack of ambition?

Surely it can't be because they are afraid of potential happiness, contentment, personal satisfaction and a sense of fulfillment.

Changing direction isn't the same thing as quitting or failure; rather, it is an acknowledgment that what you've been doing up to now isn't giving you what you want or need in life. Just because you begin your career in one field doesn't mean you can't change and do something else when you discover what your true passion is. I know a couple who were in completely unrelated fields but they shared a love of birds so they decided to open a store that sold everything to do with birds — backyard feeders, seed, tapes of bird songs, pictures, calendars, you name it. Because they were absolutely passionate about what they were doing, customers — and there are thousands of people out there who also love birds — flocked to the store, making it a tremendous success. At last count, the couple had opened two additional stores and it's easy to see that they are loving every minute of their new life.

The formula for success is far from being a secret, far from being inaccessible. It's about finding something that you love to do and then making it the focus of your career. It doesn't matter who you are, how old you are or how much you have socked away in the company pension fund, go out and do something you love to do. Feel the joy of waking up in the morning and realizing that at last you're being honest with yourself, you're no longer battling to discover a lifestyle, instead you've started to live life and you're living it your way.

Don't forget to be kind to your family when you make your move. Tell them you're sorry, but that's the way it is. "A person's gotta do what a person's gotta do!" Remarkably, you won't be damned by those who care about you. You'll be supported. "Good on you," they'll say. "I wish I had the guts to do what you're doing." And you will smile a big silly smile and feel all those tons of old, tired baggage suddenly lifted from your shoulders. You'll hold your head a little higher. And while the immediate future may be tremendously uncertain, you will walk into it knowing that it's *your* future to make and that you're doing what *you* want to do.

You have to follow your heart and do what you know to be right for you.

10

WHAT'S IN A NAME?

"Sometimes, there's more to a name
than you imagine, as I found out when
I was 12 years old."

Soon after the end of the Second World War, my parents decided
to send me to a private school for boys in East Sussex, England.
The school was in a little town called Heathfield, halfway
between what is now Royal Tunbridge Wells to the north and
the seaside town of Brighton to the south (some knowledgeable
Brits might also say that it's just down the road from Butcher's
Cross and Five Ashes. I just love the names of England's towns
and villages).

I was enrolled at a private school because my parents felt
it would afford me more opportunities in life than if I were
to attend a regular school in London. It was a big and brave
decision for my mother and father. Both were working and the
fees they would have to pay would mean huge sacrifices for both
of them. But it was one of the first big dreams that they had for
me. I would embark on the next stage of my life with a quality
education, coupled with the kind of discipline that is traditionally

part and parcel of the highly regulated private school system.

When the train left London's Victoria Station in the winter of 1947, I was just five years old and we were puffing southward into the first big adventure of my young life. I had absolutely no idea what lay ahead of me at Tavistock Hall Preparatory School for Boys in tiny Heathfield. I was an unknown quantity heading into an unpredictable future.

With me on the train that morning were other kids from London who were headed to the same destination. We sat together for the 90-minute trip, which to me at the age of five, could well have been a journey halfway around the world.

I could write a whole book just about my schoolboy adventures at Tavistock Hall, but for my purpose here, I will relate just one story. It is about an event that happened in my final year at the school and not long before the Legge family left England for a new adventure in Canada — this because my parents had decided that Canada, and specifically Vancouver, British Columbia, presented infinitely more opportunities for success than did post-war Britain. They were big dreamers and at the age of 12, I was to be part of their dream.

So it was the summer before we moved away and the annual Tavistock Sports Day was about to take place. Full of vim, vinegar and Olympian dreams, I tried out for every event on the card, but the event that I really wanted to excel in was the Half Mile for Boys. It was the glamour event and the premier race of the day — four times around the track, with the winner invariably ending up as a school hero receiving adulation of the highest order and at least 15 minutes of fame.

After the time trials, they had narrowed the contestants to a field of 15. Unfortunately for me, I hadn't made the cut. I was disappointed but thought, "What the heck?" There were plenty of other events that I could compete in and still depart from

Tavistock Hall with my head held high.

But it was not to be. Other forces were at work and things would change.

Part of the tradition at Tavistock Hall was to have the parents of boys donate trophies for specific Sports Day events (private schools do a great job getting kids started, but like every other school in the world, they always have a need for donations and support).

As luck would have it, my parents had donated a trophy for the Half Mile for Boys, which, as you already know, I hadn't qualified to participate in.

In stepped the headmaster.

There were 250 of us, all in school uniform, seated for breakfast when he arrived to deliver the news. As always happened when the "head" arrived on the scene, the hubbub ceased in an instant with not a whisper to be heard above the sea of porridge bowls that lined the table.

If you recall the scene in the breakfast hall from *Oliver Twist*, you can almost imagine how I felt as he fixed me with a stare.

"Legge," he said sternly. "You were too slow to be one of the runners in the Half Mile, but your parents have donated a trophy so I guess I'll have to put you in the race."

I was elated and scared to death all at the same moment — I would get my chance to prove myself . . . but what if I failed? It was incredible motivation for a 12-year-old boy!

Sports Day arrived and there I was at the starting line, the 16th runner in a newly augmented field. The gun went off and we ran.

At the end of the first lap I was dead last, exactly where I should have been based on the time trials. But then, as I passed the clubhouse turn, I caught the eyes of my mother, father and grandmother and I knew without a doubt that being last in the

1954 Legge Classic would not be good enough for the kid who bore the proud Legge name.

I put my 12-year-old butt in gear and began to reach out with bigger steps, a faster pace and an injection of adrenalin to get me going.

At the end of the second lap I was in 10th place and the family group had now moved to the front of their seats and were cheering me on. At the end of the third lap, I was running fifth and victory seemed entirely possible. My family was standing now and cheering wildly.

I won that race and the field of runners dropped away behind me as I plunged victoriously through the finish-line tape.

How did I win that glorious day all those years ago? I don't know exactly "how" I did it but I do know why. When my mother and father sent me to Tavistock Hall at the age of five, they did it because they believed in me and they had big dreams for me as the living legacy of the Legge family — I wasn't about to let them, or myself, down. The headmaster too, in his strange way, had provided motivation for my victory by throwing out the challenge. I needed to prove to him, and to me, that No. 16 could be No. 1.

I still have the little trophy that my mother presented to me on that very special day and a photo too, with me in my cricket whites as I stepped up to receive it.

Races aren't always exhausting physical endeavours. They can be as simple as setting a goal that you think may be just beyond your reach and then going for it. You'll be surprised how many times you can take home the prize. Whether it is earning more money, winning a new position or signing a new client — which race you choose to enter is up to you.

I have run many races since that day at Tavistock Hall — though few have taken place on a track — and many of them

I have won. What I've learned from my experience is that you never know for certain who will win until the race is over, and most races are won lap by solid lap.

As someone who has been counted out only to come back a winner, I urge you to make sure that you are there at the starting line for your race and then be sure to give it your best every step of the way and chances are, you too will be savouring sweet victory when the race is done.

You never know for certain who will win until the race is over, and most races are won lap by solid lap.

11

CONSISTENCY

Nobel Prize-winning novelist Anatole France once observed, "The average man does not know what to do with life, yet wants another one which will last forever." Rather than wish for another life, we need to focus on getting the most out of the one we have.

I recently had breakfast with Darcy Rezac, managing director of The Vancouver Board of Trade. He is also known as the Chief Engagement Officer, a fitting title for someone who has introduced his original brand of "positive networking" into the mainstream of business in Vancouver and is a guru on the techniques on this important aspect of business life. His two books on the subject, *The Frog & Prince: Secrets of Positive Networking to Change Your Life* and *Work the Pond: Use the Power of Positive Networking to Leap Forward in Work and Life*, published by Penguin Books, are both bestsellers.

As Darcy will tell you, networking requires you to "kiss a lot of frogs" (i.e., meet a lot of people) to find your "princes" — those precious few who can make a difference in your life. But the real secret to networking is discovering what you can do for someone else and Darcy's "What can I do for you?" approach has helped thousands overcome their fear of networking and find more success.

If you live or work in Vancouver, one of your stepping stones to success and power networking is to join The Board of Trade.

Here's the phone number to call: 604-681-2111. Just ask for the membership manager.

As we sat down to our breakfast that morning, Darcy said to me, "Peter, you can count on two things in life: One, you are going to lose your job; and two, you are going to die." It wasn't your usual conversation starter, but it got my attention. As breakfast continued, he went on to ask me, "What do you want written on your tombstone?"

It's the sort of question that makes you stop and think. What would I want people to remember about me, what have I accomplished and what more do I want to accomplish?

Reading Dan Sullivan and Catherine Nomura's book, *The Laws of Lifetime Growth*, I learned that only a small percentage of people are continually successful over the long run. These outstanding few recognize that every success comes as a result of the assistance they have received from many other people along the way and they are continually grateful for this support. In my mind it goes hand in hand with the law of consistency (sticking with your cause, job, career and community for life — becoming a lifer), which is one·of the most important keys to success.

Lunch that same day found me with Michael McAdams, CGA, who is the president and CEO of Teldon Printers, a $60-million employee-owned printing company based in Vancouver. They print a couple of our magazines at Canada Wide Media. Towards the end of lunch, Michael asked me, "What do you think I should do with my life/career?"

The first response that leapt to mind was "be consistent" and learn as much as you can from others. That's what I practice every day.

I've lived in the same community for 40 years — Coquitlam, B.C., Canada. I've been married to the same woman for 40 years and we've lived in the same house for 25 years. The relationships I have with my three daughters, Samantha, Rebecca and Amanda, are a priority and most people are impressed with the deep, caring connection I share with my children. I'm now working on developing a lifetime relationship with my first grandson, Benjamin David. At this writing he's just 24 months old — however, I can assure you that he is a future Nobel Prize winner.

I've been president of my company, Canada Wide Media Limited, for all of its 32 years, growing the company from one magazine to 54 magazines and online properties — today it's a $30-million organization.

I've also spent literally thousands of hours and many, many years working in the community raising money. The contribution I am probably best known for is co-hosting the *Variety Show of Hearts Telethon* for over 30 years on B.C.'s Global TV. To date, we have raised almost $140 million — with every penny dedicated to helping children in B.C. I have also established the Legge Family Scholarship and made significant contributions to Royal Roads University, the British Columbia Institute of Technology and Simon Fraser University's Segal Graduate School of Business.

No overnight success, mine has been a life of consistent performance. My chiropractor, Dr. Gohar Sheikh, once told me, "Consistency outperforms intensity."

Now you might think, "This sounds like a boring, humdrum, same-old, same-old life!"

Quite the contrary. Consider this list:

My wife Kay and I have enjoyed about 50 cruises together, visiting many places including Hawaii, Alaska, Mexico, South America and the Mediterranean. We met on a ship and our ongoing romance always seems to take us back to ships. (Here's a tip from a veteran cruiser: If you go, try to get a cabin with a balcony. It's worth it.)

I've spoken on five continents and met scores of interesting people. Kay and I interviewed the press secretary to Her Majesty Queen Elizabeth II in Buckingham Palace and then met the Queen when she visited Vancouver as part of her Golden Jubilee Celebration in 2002. I met Margaret Thatcher during Expo 86, where I was on a committee for the British Pavilion along with my mentor, Ray Addington. The pavilion hosted a private reception for Mrs. Thatcher and Kay and I both attended.

I have spoken in the House of Commons in Ottawa at a prayer breakfast.

I visited the White House — I was speaking for the H.Y. Louie company and they arranged a private tour.

In 2004, I was chair of The Vancouver Board of Trade, which took both Kay and me to the World Economic Forum in Davos, Switzerland, where I met Queen Noor of Jordan, along with many other influential people from around the world.

My daughter Rebecca and I had a private lunch with HRH Prince and Princess Michael of Kent in Kensington Palace.

As I continue to enjoy my speaking career and build my company, my list continues to grow. Your list of highlights may be quite different from mine, but you need to keep adding to it as well. The important thing is to be passionate about what you are doing and maintain a balance between what you want for yourself and what you can do to help others.

Here are the things that I focus on to keep my life balanced:
• Consistency of vision
• Having a strong work ethic
• Looking out for others
• Providing encouragement rather than criticism
• Being passionate about what I do
• Perseverance in reaching goals

• Taking care of my staff and those who have helped me (because I know that I can't do it all on my own).

So, what would you say in answer to Darcy Rezac's question? What do *you* want it to say on your tombstone? Thomas Edison once said that if we were able to do all the things we are capable of doing, we would literally astonish ourselves.

Get ready to be astonished.

"If you have faith, as a grain of mustard seed, nothing shall be impossible unto you."
— Matthew 17:20

12

THE SUPER SIX

I'm on another long airplane ride from Vancouver to Toronto so I'm searching through my carry-on for my latest book acquisition. James Arthur Ray's book, *Harmonic Wealth*, caught my attention at the airport bookstore so I picked it up.

While I have read about him in other books and magazines, Ray's retelling of the story of Charles M. Schwab, the president of Bethlehem Steel, leapt out at me and it makes an important point that is worth including here.

At the turn of the last century, a man named Ivy Lee met with Charles M. Schwab, president of Bethlehem Steel. His objective was to sell his services to Schwab and help his company become more efficient. Schwab's reaction to Lee's proposal was that his people already knew what they should be doing — his real problem was simply one of getting them to do it. As a result, Schwab wasn't buying.

"Just suppose I could give you a tool, an action that would guarantee you'd become more efficient, you'd be interested, wouldn't you?" Lee asked. "Better yet," he continued, sensing Schwab's resistance, "how about if I just give you the idea — let you use it for 21 days and if it works, you share it with your employees. Then send me a cheque for whatever you think it's worth."

"Well, okay, what is it?" Schwab asked.

"At the beginning of every single day, or better yet, at the end of the day before the following day, take out a piece of paper and write down the six most important things you need to do to achieve your objectives on that particular day," Lee said. "In fact, go ahead and do that right now for tomorrow." Schwab thought about it, and wrote down six action items.

"Now put them in order of importance, one being the most important, two being the second most important, and so on," Lee continued. So Schwab did that.

"Starting tomorrow first thing, start on item number one. Do not go on to item number two until you have fully completed item number one. Then continue in succession with each number. If you get to the end of the day and have not completed your full list of action items, then roll over your actions to the next day. If five and six are left one day, they automatically become items one and two for the next. Use this for as long as you like, and then if you think it's worth something, send me a cheque for that amount."

Less than a month later, Ivy Lee got a cheque in the mail for the then-princely sum of $25,000. Attached was a note signed by Charles M. Schwab that read:

"That's the most powerful tool for achievement that anyone has ever taught me and here's a fraction of what it's worth."

Although Bethlehem Steel was relatively unknown at the time, it would go on to become the largest steel producer in the world within five years and Charles Schwab would earn $100,000 on his own, making him the most powerful and famous steel man alive. The $25,000 investment he made in Ivy Lee's idea turned into many millions at a time when the average income in the American workforce was around two dollars a day.

"Since then, many powerful business people have attributed their success to this technique," writes James Arthur Ray in his book. "So, if it's good enough for them, guess what I'm going to ask you to do every day, starting today? Uh huh. Do what I call your Critical Six, but only if you want to skyrocket your results. If not, don't bother."

I have been using this same technique in my own life for 15 years and it is something that I have shared with everyone who works at Canada Wide Media because it can be used to keep you focused on what's really important in all areas of your life. I like to call it my Super Six.

Start today by writing down the six most important things you need to accomplish right now . . . and then get going.

13

IT TAKES TIME TO BECOME
AN OVERNIGHT SENSATION

Not long ago, my wife Kay and I spent a few days in New York City where I was doing a speaking engagement. While we were there we went to see the *Jersey Boys*, a theatrical production based on the story of Frankie Valli and the Four Seasons. Hailing from New Jersey, the Four Seasons were the reigning royalty of Italian singing groups throughout the '60s and '70s and became a world-class act whose popularity spread throughout North America and across the ocean to Europe. Their sound, which combined elements of doo wop and R&B in addition to other pre-rock vocal styles, provided the soundtrack for young people growing up on the East Coast in the same way that their contemporaries, the Beach Boys, did for those living on the West Coast.

What I didn't know was that before he became famous, Frankie Valli had four or five different groups — including the Variatones, Frankie Valley and the Travelers, the Four Lovers and Frankie Valli and the Romans — and changed his name more times than Elizabeth Taylor got married during the same period of time.

As with so many other "overnight sensations," Frankie's life was not without its trials, tribulations, heartbreaks and failures, but he always stayed focused on his goal of performing and recording hit songs. Along with his musical partner, Bob Gaudio, he also knew how to keep reinventing his music to appeal to record buyers. During their two decades at the top of the music charts, Frankie Valli and the Four Seasons had 46 singles that made it onto the charts, sold over $85 million worth of records and went through several changes in band members while still managing to stay true to who they were. Some of their hit songs through the years included: *Big Girls Don't Cry*; *Walk Like a Man*; *Bye, Bye, Baby*; *Working My Way Back to You*; *My Eyes Adored You*; and *Grease.*

There's an old saying, the harder you work, the luckier you get. Becoming an overnight sensation usually involves years, if not decades of hard work, practice and even failure. Just ask anyone who is or has been one and they'll tell you. Of course, hard work and perseverance aren't very sexy in the eyes of the media, and that's why the lean years so often get glossed over in the telling of success stories.

The cold hard truth is that it takes discipline and dedication to turn your back on the idea that there are secrets or shortcuts to success and it takes true, rock-steady commitment to continuously focus on working towards your goals day by day and have faith that the cumulative impact will be worth the effort. As Frankie Valli and the Four Seasons proved time and again throughout their musical career, that *is* the secret to success.

Do you dream of being the next overnight
sensation in your field of endeavour?
Get to work and start taking small steps
towards your goal today.

"There are no unrealistic goals
— just unrealistic deadlines."
— Brian Tracy

14

POBODY'S NERFECT

In my book *The Runway of Life*, I tell the story of my first entrepreneurial adventure as the operator of a hot-dog stand at the Pacific National Exhibition (PNE), Vancouver's long-running annual end-of-summer fair. Like many would-be business owners, I started out with visions of grandeur, thinking that it was an opportunity to make some easy money.

At the time, I already had a full-time job at *The Columbian* newspaper in New Westminster, B.C., but I wanted to purchase a second car for my wife. The problem was that at my current earning capacity, a car for Kay was likely still several years away.

Enter the business opportunity. Some associates of mine were selling a concession stand that they had run at the PNE the previous year. It was called "Bunny's Foot Long Hot Dogs." At the time, foot-long hot dogs were all the rage and from the financials they showed me, it seemed a very easy 17-day venture that would enable me to buy that second car.

For a modest amount, I purchased the hot-dog stand and became the proud owner of my very first venture. And that's where the problems started, problems that I hadn't even begun to think about before I handed over the money. For starters, I had no idea who was going to manage this little enterprise. I also hadn't thought about where I would find suppliers, how I would pay for inventory or where we would get the staff to run the stand from morning to night.

We eventually decided that my wife would be the one to run the stand — and I know *you* saw this coming, but at the time, with visions of easy money in my head, I didn't — that created the biggest problem of all. How was my wife going to get to the PNE every day without a car?

With no other choice, we bit the bullet and paid $475 in cash for an Austin 1100 (a considerable sum of money at the time) before we had sold even a single hot dog. So much for planning ahead.

Unfortunately, the comedy of errors didn't end there. Running a hot-dog concession at a fair is more work than you'd think. As a result, my mom, dad and I ended up working alongside my wife for 17 days straight from 10 a.m. to midnight. On top of that, because we couldn't afford a babysitter, we also brought along our young daughter Samantha.

In the end, I think that Samantha must have eaten our profits because when the fair was over and the smell of grilled hot dogs had finally been washed from our clothes, we barely broke even. The good news is that Kay got her car and I was more than happy to return to my job at the newspaper . . . at least until the next big idea came along.

Now, reading this story you might think that the lesson I should have taken away from this adventure would be to stick to my day job and leave the business ventures to those who have more discretionary money to work with or more business expertise, but I beg to disagree. The best lessons come from our failures, not our successes.

Our culture advertises perfection and unfortunately, many of us fall into the trap of trying to live up to an impossible standard. But who do you know that is perfect? Everyone has challenges to overcome. It's how we navigate through those challenges that will determine our success in life. That's why it is important to set your own goals and focus on what will bring *you* real happiness, not what is expected of you or what others think you should be doing.

Being genuine is more important than being perfect. It's also more satisfying because it doesn't require you to act like someone you're not. In my case, I had a strong entrepreneurial spirit that just needed to find the right opportunity. Eventually I did and as a result I took a single fledgling magazine and built it into a thriving publishing company that not only brings me great satisfaction, but also provides me with the opportunity to work with two of my lovely and talented daughters. What could be better than that? I'm glad I didn't worry about what other people thought I should be doing with my life!

So if you find yourself struggling to keep up with the Joneses or trying to keep up appearances with your friends, neighbours or colleagues, it's probably time to re-evaluate your approach to life. By taking a chance on me, I learned a great deal that summer, primarily that entrepreneurship isn't about the "perfect opportunity." It is about passion, challenge, creativity and using the resources at hand.

Here are a few other lessons I would like to share:

People will tell you what you *can't* do; they won't tell you what you *can* do.
The world is full of critics. More often than not, the people who spend their time telling others what can't be done are problem finders, not problem solvers. They would rather be spectators than active participants. Likewise, most times the people who have accomplished something significant in their own lives are the first to encourage you to do the same. These are the people to seek out for guidance and advice on your endeavours.

Don't follow the leader, be the leader.
If you truly want to be an entrepreneur, you must look for opportunity where others see only obstacles and strike out in your own direction. When you achieve a goal that was once thought unattainable, you provide the impetus for others to dream bigger, work harder and go further. For example, Roger Bannister was the first runner to break the four-minute mile when many said it couldn't be done. Today, the four-minute mile is standard in competition simply because he proved that it *could* be done. What's your four-minute mile?

Expect resistance and learn to push through it.
Entrepreneurs are constantly challenging the world to accept new ideas and using these ideas to improve society. In essence, they are out to change the world and that can scare a lot of people. To succeed, you must be ready to answer this resistance and respond by demonstrating the value of your ideas again and again.

Carpe Diem.
If you've seen the movie *Dead Poets Society*, you'll be familiar with this lesson. In the movie, as a teacher at an exclusive boys' school, Mr. Keating tells his students, "Don't wait until it's too late to realize your potential. Carpe Diem — Seize the Day! To know you have lived with meaning, to know you have existed with purpose, and to know you brought life to your passions . . . then you can say, 'Yes, I seized the day.' "

Entrepreneurship isn't about
the "perfect opportunity." It is about
passion, challenge, creativity
and using the resources at hand.

15

LEADERSHIP SECRETS OF
THE SALVATION ARMY

William Booth, founder of The Salvation Army, was once asked to telegraph his officers using just one word to describe what The Salvation Army is all about. After much thought, the one simple word that he came up with was, "OTHERS."

"It is not about us," he said, "It's about others."

The Salvation Army has been true to this one word for over 100 years in Canada — helping the needy, the sick, the downtrodden and the disheartened. The book *Leadership Secrets of The Salvation Army*, written by the former Commissioner of The Salvation Army in the United States, Robert Watson, captures the real essence of leadership as one of service to others.

The Salvation Army's military style is rooted in the militaristic spirit that was prevalent in the mid-1800s, when William Booth and his wife Catherine began their work in London, England. This organizational style has proven effective in making the Army a highly disciplined and mobile organization, able to respond quickly and efficiently to human need whenever and wherever it arises. Today, The Salvation Army's uniform is recognized as a symbol of commitment and a sign of availability and accessibility in times of need or crisis.

Peter Drucker once said, "The Salvation Army is by far the most effective organization in the United States. No one even comes close to it with respect to clarity of mission, ability to innovate, measurable results, dedication, and putting money to maximum use."

The fact that The Salvation Army is one of only two organizations that were around when the Dow Jones started in 1884 and still in existence today is a testament to the strength of purpose of this organization.

When William Booth died on August 20, 1912, at the age of 83, 40,000 people filled the auditorium to pay their respects. Monarchs sent wreaths and behind the funeral cortege, 5,000 members of the famed and highly respected Salvation Army marched six abreast. Even Queen Mary, an admirer of Booth and his work, chose at the last minute to attend. Because of her late decision, however, no special place of honour had been arranged for her and she took her place among the common folk of England. Finding herself seated in a sea of people, the queen soon discovered that she was sitting next to a one-time prostitute whom Booth had told shortly before his death, "One day, when you get to heaven, you'll have a place of honour."

So how did this one man leave behind an organization so prepared for the future that it could continue growing strong nearly 100 years after his death, recently attracting the largest single charitable donation — $2 billion — in history? In *Leadership Secrets of The Salvation Army*, Robert Watson shares the principles that have made The Salvation Army so effective in the U.S., Canada and around the world. These include the following five laws that would make any organization more productive and efficient:

1. Clarity of Mission — The Salvation Army uses a laser-like focus to evaluate everything it does in terms of its mission of preaching the gospel and meeting human needs without discrimination.

2. Ability to Innovate — The Salvation Army's investment in

people gets incredible returns making it as much "venture capitalist" as it is charity.

3. Measurable Results — The Army has developed a unique way of setting, monitoring and celebrating the achievement of measurable goals that allows it to say, "Look, we promised we would do this and we delivered."

4. Dedication — It's how The Army accomplishes so much with a relatively small cadre of officers.

5. Putting Money to Maximum Use — The Army's bare skeleton of a national organization makes the most of every resource and ensures that each operational unit is self-sufficient.

What are the laws that govern your business?

How could you apply the secrets
of The Salvation Army to make your
organization more effective?

16

MR. CONDO'S PRINCIPLES OF SUCCESS

Earlier in this book I talked about how I told a group of second- and third-year students at The Sauder School of Business at the University of British Columbia that there are actually no "secrets" to success and how, instead, life has a way of rewarding those who work hard, study, apply principles of success, naturally have a positive attitude and take full responsibility for their future and actions.

Sir Isaac Newton once said, "I've learned so much because I have stood on the shoulders of giants."

I've met and interviewed many of Vancouver's business giants. Among them is Bob Rennie, who is affectionately referred to as "Mr. Condo" for his prowess in the real estate marketing business. We had lunch at the Four Seasons Hotel recently and my impression from that meeting is that it would be difficult to come across a more likeable, affable man.

The reason we were having lunch in the first place was that my company had featured Bob Rennie on the March 2008 cover of *BCBusiness Magazine* — which, incidentally, was voted magazine of the year by the Western Magazine Foundation — and I wanted to meet him in person. I wasn't disappointed. He was kind, open, interesting, focused, relaxed and he made the 90-minute lunch absolutely fly by as I peppered him with questions about his career selling real estate.

From my lunch notes, I extracted seven principles that Bob

employs in his business to be successful. Here's his list:

1. "We are valued by the size of our Rolodex, our contact list," he says. Therefore, get out and network whenever you can, make connections.
2. "I get up at 4:45 a.m., seven days a week, and the first 15 minutes I use to plan my day," says Bob. The lesson: get an early start and know what you want to accomplish each day.
3. "I keep a tight and organized scheduled and I am in control of my day," Bob explains. Which means, schedule what you need to do each day and then stick with it.
4. "No drinking at all — ever," says Bob emphatically. He explains that it is important for him to be sharp and on his game at all times and alcohol would get in the way of that.
5. "My one luxury is I have a car and driver. It might look excessive, but it's one of the best business decisions I have ever made. It keeps me organized," he says. The nugget here: if you're going to indulge, make it something that adds real value to your life.
6. "Some people call me an instant success — but it took 35 years," says Bob. If you want to be an "overnight success," you'd better be prepared to work hard to make it happen, because it definitely takes longer than most people think.
7. "For my sanity and survival, I collect contemporary art, paintings, sculptures and illustrations. I have about 1,000 pieces from around the world," Bob tells me. The reality check: you can't put all of your energy into work; having another passion in your life helps to provide balance.

"Some people call me an
instant success — but it took 35 years."
— Bob Rennie

17

MAKE A GOOD IMPRESSION

People will make a decision on you in the first four seconds. It's not my statistic, but I think it's pretty accurate. The way you dress, your tie, your attitude, your haircut, your sense of style, whether or not you look them in the eyes when you speak, your handshake, your manners, it's a lot for someone to take in — but they do it and that four-second impression can have a lasting effect on what they think of you.

My father told me that one of the most important aspects to pay attention to in making your four-second impression is your shoes, because it is your shoes that people will see both when you are approaching them and when you are walking away. Take a moment to look at your own shoes. What do you see? Are they in good repair, clean, shiny and presentable or are they dull, scuffed and in need of some tender loving care?

Now your wardrobe and shoes don't have to be expensive, just smart and well tailored. I got several of my favourite suits for less than $200 — by picking them up at Macy's when they were having a big sale during one of my many business trips.

In honour of my father, who always looked impeccably turned out and took excellent care of his shoes, here are some shoeshine tips from three of the best:

Penny Simmons — The ex-stockbroker and owner of Toronto's Penny Loafers Shoe Shine Company advises, "Don't wipe your shoes with water. Saddle soap is the best cleaner, and the cleaner the shoe, the better the results. For salt stains, just keep a sachet of white vinegar on you, and in a pinch, you can use nail polish remover to remove scuff marks from patent leather."

Drew Goodall — The owner of London's Sunshine Shoeshine and winner of Best Shoeshine in the 2007 British Shoeshine Championships has this to say, "Alternate your shoes three times a week and use shoe trees made of a light wood such as cedar. If you use one of those magic sponge all-in-ones, it's like whitening your teeth but not really cleaning them. They have a lot of silicone, which gives shoes the shine but doesn't nourish the leather. Opt for natural wax instead."

Allan Feaster — The winner of the vote for San Francisco's Best Shoe Shine by *SF Weekly* offers this tip, "I call people who put polish straight on the shoe, shoe murderers. Use a cream first and then the polish."

Good impressions are like seeds — once you plant them it's surprising how quickly they can grow into something wonderful.

BEING YOUR BEST

18

MAKE SURE YOUR COMPETENCE
SHINES THROUGH

My friend and fellow speaker Mark Sanborn travels a great deal to give presentations all over North America and beyond. One of the major themes that Mark talks about in his speeches is developing your level of competence in doing the job that you do, no matter what that might be. It is also an important part of his new book, *You Don't Need a Title to Be a Leader*. That concept is beautifully illustrated in the following story taken from his book.

Mark writes, "There are few pleasures I enjoy more in life than a good shoeshine. While changing planes in Detroit recently, I decided to get my shoes shined. But before deciding whether or not to give the shoeshine guy my business, I watched him for a few minutes to determine the quality of his work.

"The shoe I watched him shine looked terrific, so I decided to give him a try. As he worked, I commented on the quality of the shoeshines I had received at other airports, mentioning how difficult it was to gauge the kind of shoeshine I would get in places where I hadn't been before.

"Hearing this, the fellow stopped what he was doing and looked up at me with astonishment. 'It's easy to tell if you're going to get a good shine,' he told me. 'Just look at the shoes of the guy giving the shine.

'If they ain't fine, walk on by!'

I glanced at his shoes. They literally shone. They were a walking billboard proclaiming his competence."

What are you currently doing to build competence in the different areas of your life?

How can you make sure that your competence shines through?

19

ASK THREE TIMES AND FLICK ONCE

In my book *Who Dares Wins*, I devote a chapter to Canadian astronaut Julie Payette, whom I met at a St. John Ambulance luncheon where she was giving a presentation on her experience aboard the Space Shuttle Discovery and a mission to the International Space Station in 1999.

One point that she made during her speech that really caught my attention was about how critical both planning and teamwork are to the success of the space program. As an example, Julie told us that in space no switch is flicked (or any other action carried out) until the action has been cleared three times by another crew member — it's a policy that takes the old carpenter's adage, "measure twice, cut once," to a whole new level, and rightly so. After all, in space, making even a small mistake can have deadly consequences.

"It is also absolutely vital that the entire crew work together as one," Julie explained. To ensure that she was prepared for her mission, prior to her space assignment, Julie was required to study and understand Russian to ensure that she would be able to communicate effectively aboard the International Space Station.

Was it easy?

Nyet!

But, as Julie told us, it did help to bring together a diverse group of astronauts from different countries and make them into an efficient space *team*.

In addition to her comments on teamwork, Julie also talked about the level of planning that goes into every facet of the space program. Here on earth, we talk about plans and sometimes we develop reasonably *good* plans, but we also know that if things go wrong, we can always start over or at least have another try at it. In space, you don't get a second chance when big things go wrong. You can't call 911 in space, you can't open the window for more air and you can't say, "Hey, it didn't work, but we'll get around to fixing the problem later."

Imagine if your life depended on being absolutely sure that you would get it right the first time . . . and every time.

Just think of the time and energy we could probably save if we took just a little extra care to plan and prepare before we put the gears in motion. The problem is that we often think that we know more than we do. And that, says Julie Payette, is probably the greatest fault that we all share as human beings. "We delude ourselves into believing that we have great knowledge," she says. "But when you're looking at the earth from space, you realize just how very little we actually understand about our world and how much there is to learn."

Julie knows that she is one of the lucky few. As astronauts, she and her colleagues have been given a unique perspective on this place we call "spaceship earth." They see our blue oceans, our green forests, our snow-capped mountains and our vast stretches of desert. But they also see the things that have gone wrong, the horrible mistakes that have smudged our planet, maybe forever. Hopefully, we will have the opportunity to correct some of those mistakes, but if not, at the very least we can and should learn from them so that we don't repeat them.

I kept my notes from Julie's presentation because "ask three times, flick once," makes a lot of sense to me — and it may just be the philosophy we need to tackle some of the toughest global issues facing us today.

In what areas of your life would it be beneficial to apply the principle "ask three times and flick once"?

20

EVERYTHING COUNTS

In the many years that I have been a professional speaker talking to audiences around the globe, a consistent theme in my presentations is that in life, absolutely everything counts. From the moment that we are born until the day that we check out of Hotel Earth for the last time, we are shaped by our surroundings — our home environment; our education; what we choose to read, listen to and watch; the friends and acquaintances we associate with; our workplace environment; our life partners; the neighbours who surround us and the communities we belong to — and as a result, the quality of everything we see and do contributes to the evolving beings that we are.

When I think of the implications of this, it reminds me of the computer term *Garbage In, Garbage Out*, which was coined to keep early computer programmers mindful of the fact that the applications they produced would only be as good as the planning and data that went into creating them. It's a good guiding principle that each one of us can use to determine what we allow into our life.

In addition to the idea that everything counts, I also talk about action and reaction and about reaping what we sow. Socrates observed that for every cause there is at least one effect. It is simple, beautiful wisdom: everything counts and it is up to us to determine how much our life will count for. If we wish, we can go passively through life letting the influences of the world wash over us. We can also, if we choose, be completely unaware that we're part of anything at all. You've met people like this. You can talk to them about all kinds of frivolous things, but try to take the conversation to a deeper level and you hit a dead end.

"I don't watch the news and I don't read the papers," they will say. "There's enough misery in this world without me having to know about it."

"Vote? No, I never vote. No matter what happens in an election, the same bad actors always get back in."

"Give to a worthy cause? I believe that charity begins at home."

"Go back to school? What for? I know plenty of people who have more than one degree and they still can't get a decent job."

I find that people who think in these terms are tremendously draining on the rest of us. If only they would realize that taking other directions in life can offer such wonderfully fulfilling rewards. The catch is that it's a choice that each person needs to make for him or herself.

To help determine whether their choices are taking them in the right direction, I often suggest to my audiences that they do a features and benefits assessment of themselves. This involves looking at the various areas of your life and applying a rating — on a scale of one to 10 — of how well you are doing. For instance, if you get along well with people, give yourself an eight in that area. However, if you get along exceptionally well with others, give yourself a 10. What about follow-through? Do you follow up with tasks and responsibilities in a timely and effective manner? If so, you'll want to rate yourself at the high end of the scale. In this manner, we would proceed through a list of attributes that we all believe are essential to being a well-rounded person and that would most likely contribute to success in life.

When we do this assessment, what we discover along the way — if we're honest, and why wouldn't we be? — is that all of us find some areas where we are wanting. And more often than not it is because we have let the little things slip, things such as maintaining a healthy weight, spending quality time with our spouse or children, getting enough exercise and rest, broadening our knowledge, participating in community activities and so on.

If we don't conduct this type of inventory from time to time and make adjustments to our behaviour, we will soon discover that the accumulation of little things will begin to affect our quality of life in a negative way — causing us to drift away from loved ones; get ill more often than we used to; be unable to participate in important discussions about topics that should be in our knowledge inventory; or find that we are disconnected from our community. It's a horrible thought, but we begin to resemble those self-absorbed individuals we say that we abhor.

How can we keep this from happening?

Life is complex and at times, difficult. We need guiding principles to keep us headed in the direction we want to travel. When we don't have these, it's easy to get bogged down by even the smallest of details. Garbage in, garbage out!

In more than 10 years of doing business, I have learned that everything functions much better in my world when I'm working to a plan and I can align all of the different areas of my life according to the goals and ideals that I have set out for myself. Having a plan and doing a regular personal assessment inventory are just two of the guiding principles that help me to stay on track.

They can help you too. Start by doing a personal assessment inventory now to determine where you're at in different areas of your life. Based on your assessment, you can see which areas you need to work on and plan how you will make changes to improve your score. If you don't already have both short- and longer-term goals written down, it's a good time to do that as well.

After a few months, do another assessment to measure your progress. If you set yourself a short-term goal, have you reached it? If you said that you would investigate a career change, what have you done to move in that direction? If you're not happy with your level of physical activity, what changes have you made in your behaviour?

This exercise works best if you keep a record of your progress and make a commitment to be really honest. Remember, you don't have to answer to anyone but yourself, but who could be better at asking the right questions?

The quality of everything we see and do contributes to the evolving beings that we are.

21

A FORMULA FOR FAILURE

In volume three of my series *If Only I'd Said That*, I include a short piece written by Jim Rohn on the formula for failure. As Jim explains in the article, failure in life isn't the result of one cataclysmic event, but rather the effect of an accumulation of poor choices and bad decisions over a long period of time.

For example, those who regularly eat foods that are highly processed and full of sugar, sodium and saturated fats are contributing to future health problems, but the joy of the moment greatly overshadows any consequences that may come in the future, so they continue to overindulge. It's the same for people who continue to smoke, take drugs or drink to excess year after year. More than likely, they continue to do it because the consequences of their actions aren't immediate and therefore they think it doesn't matter.

As Jim Rohn points out, "Failure's most dangerous attribute is its subtlety." In the short term, all of those little errors and poor choices don't seem to make any difference, so we let them slide. And with no immediate consequences to capture our attention, we continue to drift from one day to the next making wrong choices and repeating those mistakes until the day we finally wake up and realize we have a much bigger problem on our hands.

That's the formula for failure and it can be applied to almost everything we do, whether it is failing to communicate with our spouse, failing to spend time and guide our children as they grow or failing to serve our customers and invest in the growth of our business. The best way to inoculate ourselves from failure is to realize that the little choices we make every day — such as how to spend our free time, who we associate with and how we feed our mind, body and soul — all of these choices matter, and they matter a lot in the long term.

Here are some guidelines that I use to stay on the right track:

Exercise — Try to dedicate at least 20 minutes a day to physical activity. Play soccer with the kids, go for a walk with your spouse, take the stairs, enjoy a short bike ride. Whatever it takes, move your body and you will feel it respond with more energy. Exercise is also an excellent way to reduce stress and increase overall well-being.

Read good books — Charlie Tremendous Jones has said, "You will be the same person you are today in five years except for the people you meet, the places you go and the books you read." Good books uplift and inspire us. I make an effort to read at least one book every week and as a result I get a lot of my best ideas from books. The trick is to not just read the book and put it back on the shelf. The knowledge found in books is there to be used — and shared — I mark up the books I read so that I can refer back to the important bits later. I also like to include what I have learned in my speeches and presentations and share it with friends and colleagues.

Watch what you eat — Literally! Don't mindlessly grab that bag of snack chips, sit down on the couch and eat the whole thing. Proper nourishment is the key to a healthy mind and body.

Strive for a balanced diet and choose fresh food over packaged whenever possible. Smaller portions and more frequent meals also help to ward off unhealthy cravings. If you eat well and feel good, you'll be much better prepared to deal with all of the challenges that come your way.

Focus on building relationships — You're not the only one facing challenges. Talk to people, ask questions and share your own experiences. When we feel connected with others we are less inclined to indulge in self-destructive behaviour. We are also more likely to ask for help when we need it and listen to good advice when it is given.

"Failure is not a single, cataclysmic event.
We do not fail overnight. Failure
is the inevitable result of an accumulation
of poor thinking and poor choices."
— Jim Rohn

22

SIMPLICITY IN ALL THINGS

Despite the fact that we live in a complicated and technological age, it's interesting to note that some of the most successful technology companies around are those who subscribe to the KISS principle, as in "Keep It Simple, Stupid." Google is a good example of this. Perhaps the biggest reason why Google has been so successful is that they have a very simple and very specific goal. From the beginning, founders Larry Page and Sergey Brin focused on gathering information from around the Internet and then allowing people to access the best of that information without having to sift through piles and piles of content to find what they were looking for.

The Google homepage, with a simple input box and two search buttons, is itself a testament to the KISS principle. It's so simple that even a preschooler can use it. You type in what you are looking for, hit the search button and it delivers. Because the program is intuitive, you don't even have to spell words correctly to get the results you want. I love the way that Marissa Mayer, Google's director of consumer Web products, describes what her company does: "Google has the functionality of a really complicated Swiss Army knife, but the home page is our way of approaching it closed. It's simple, it's elegant, you can slip it in your pocket, but it's got the great doodad when you need it."

Interestingly, it was by accident that the original Google homepage had such a simple design. With both founders consumed with writing code for their new search engine, Sergey Brin simply wanted to hack together something that could be used to send queries to the back end where the cool technology was. Because they didn't have a webmaster and he was unable to do HTML himself, Brin made a barebones design and stuck it in place. Once they realized that the simplicity of their user interface offered a huge competitive advantage in the market, it became the backbone of their corporate philosophy.

Today, the Google search engine has become so popular that the word "google" has been adopted into our everyday language to describe the act of using a search engine to find information; as in, "If you want to know about the history of Canada, why don't you just google it?"

What can we learn from Google? Simple is beautiful, in business and in life. This principle, which is commonly referred to as Ockham's Razor in the world of science and mathematics, is used extensively to remind theoreticians that when presented with multiple competing theories that would explain a phenomenon or solve a problem, all other things being equal, the simplest solution is the best. The theory is named after William of Ockham, a 14th-century philosopher, and it is something that I try to practice every day.

If you want to simplify your own life but don't know how to get started, here are a few tips:

1. Make a list of the top four or five things that are most important in your life. What do you value most? Simplifying starts with choosing your priorities.
2. Evaluate your commitments. Next, take a look at everything you've got going on in your life right now — from your job to your family, volunteer work, kids' activities, hobbies and community involvement. Think about which ones add value to your life and which ones you love to do.

How do they line up with the priorities you identified in step number one? Keep the ones that support your priorities and drop the rest.

3. Evaluate how you spend your time. What things do you do from the time you wake up to the time you go to sleep? How much of your time each day is spent focusing on your priorities? Redesign your daily routine to focus on what's important.

4. Simplify tasks. At home and at work, choose to work smarter, not harder. Whenever possible, automate, eliminate, delegate or hire help to take care of tasks that need to be done, but aren't high on your priority list.

5. Learn to say no. It is far more effective and practical to give your full attention to a few priority projects than to say yes to everything that comes your way. Make a point not to say yes to a new commitment until you have evaluated it in terms of the priorities you have set for yourself. Be steadfast in your resolve and soon you will find you have more time for what you truly love to do.

Simple is beautiful, in business and in life.

23

REVISIT THE 80/20 RULE

I've been reading the new book by John Maxwell called *Leadership Gold*. In it he has taken the 80/20 rule (also known as the Pareto Principle) to a different level. Eighty per cent of the traffic jams, he writes, occur on 20 per cent of the roads; 80 per cent of all beer is consumed by 20 per cent of beer drinkers.

Reading his book — which, by the way, is filled with great lessons — reminded me of the value of the Pareto Principle as a tool for focusing our attention on what is really important: the 20 per cent.

- 80 per cent of concessions will be made in the last 20 per cent of negotiations.
- 80 per cent of sales will be made in the last 20 per cent of your presentation.
- 80 per cent of your income will come from 20 per cent of your clients.

This is so true.

How can we use this information to become more effective every day?

If you're not happy with the results you're getting in your life, you need to change the 20 per cent that you're focusing on and re-evaluate what is important to you.

"Control your destiny or someone else will," says Jack Welch, former president and chair of General Electric in his book, *Jack: Straight From the Gut.*

By identifying the 20 per cent that you want to focus on and that will bring you the results you want, you can prioritize your efforts and eliminate the trivial things that take up your time and slow your progress. It's not unlike clearing out your sock drawer and throwing out the socks that have holes in them. Think about it, if 80 per cent of your socks have holes in them and yet you keep washing them and putting them back in the drawer with the 20 per cent that don't, how much time are you going to waste every day trying to find two socks without any holes?

You wouldn't keep old socks when you could easily replace them with new ones, so why would you keep doing things elsewhere in your life that don't produce the results you want?

If you're having trouble figuring out which 20 per cent is producing results, try this little exercise. Make a table with one column that lists all of the tasks you do every day. In the next column, write down how much time you spend on each task (for example, one hour answering emails, two hours following up with clients, one hour commuting, etc.). In a third column, estimate what percentage you believe each activity contributes to your overall productivity (how critical is it to your success?). Once you have determined a value for each, decide how you can eliminate, simplify or delegate the items that contribute a low percentage so that you can focus on items that contribute a high percentage.

I first heard about the 80/20 rule from fellow speaker Brian Tracy, who advises that you should always focus on performing the most valuable tasks. "The most valuable tasks you can do each day are often the hardest and most complex. But the payoff and rewards for completing these tasks efficiently can be tremendous. For this reason, you must adamantly refuse to work on tasks in the bottom 80 per cent while you still have tasks in the top 20 per cent left to be done. Before you begin work, always ask yourself, 'Is this task in the top 20 per cent of my activities or in the bottom 80 per cent?' "

It's not only important to do things right, but also to ensure you're doing the right things.

24

LET GO OF CLUTTER

We've all heard the saying that cleanliness is next to godliness. I believe that the same can be said for keeping your life free from clutter. Og Mandino puts it beautifully in the following quote which speaks about our actions as well as the possessions we accumulate, "Never again clutter your days or nights with so many menial and unimportant things that you have no time to accept a real challenge when it comes along. This applies to play as well as work. A day merely survived is no cause for celebration. You are not here to fritter away your precious hours when you have the ability to accomplish so much by making a slight change in your routine. No more busy work. No more hiding from success. Leave time, leave space, to grow. Now. Now! Not tomorrow!"

My main mentor in life, Joe Segal, once told me, "If you don't need something, rather than hold onto it, give it to someone who does." For many of us, it's easy to say, but hard to do and that's exactly why you, like many people, may have an old couch, bed or other piece of furniture stored in the basement. Although you put it there thinking that one day you might need it when you turn the space into a games room or one of the kids might want it when they finally move out on their own, in your heart, you know that eventually you'll most likely have to pay someone to take it away. Yet it's still there year after year and now it's covered with other things that you might use someday, taking up space and making it less likely that you will ever use the space for anything other than storage.

It's amazing how attached we have become to all of "our stuff" as comedian George Carlin called it in his famous stand-up routine. The scary part is that for many people it's really getting out of control. The June 23, 2008, edition of *Maclean's* magazine did a story on North America's fastest-growing real estate segment, the storage business, which generates $22 billion per year in revenue. In fact, in the span of just one decade, the amount of this kind of storage space in the United States has more than doubled to an area larger than the total land mass of Manhattan and San Francisco combined!

Interestingly, the article noted that many of the people who rent these storage lockers have a greater volume of "stuff" in storage than they have in their own homes and they are paying money to keep it there because they don't have room to put it anywhere else — because of all their other "stuff." Imagine how much easier (and less complicated) their lives would be if they got rid of some of that stuff.

So what part of your life needs tidying up? Is it your car, your desk at work, your computer hard drive, that drawer or closet where you put everything that doesn't have a place? Maybe it's all of these.

Clearing out the clutter in your life doesn't just get rid of old junk that gets in the way, it also frees up your mind and creates room for you to move forward with important plans and goals. So don't store your stuff, make a decision on what can stay and what needs to go and then take action. When you've rid your life of clutter — by cleaning out the trunk of your car, organizing your desk or finally letting go of all that stuff you had stored in the basement — suddenly you'll have a much clearer view of everything that you do have and feel infinitely more productive in your space with room to think and breathe.

Helpful Tips to Rid Your Life of Clutter

Start with nothing and add only what you need. This is a very effective way to remove unnecessary clutter. Rather than looking at things to throw away, imagine that the room or space was completely bare and then only add what you really need. This is a great way to decide whether a thing is of practical importance or just there out of habit.

Don't just de-clutter; organize. Sometimes it is not just a matter of throwing things away, you also need to get organized. First, find a convenient spot for everything that you use on a regular basis and make sure it's kept there. Once that's done, you can put the items that are rarely used but still necessary in a less handy spot like the garage or a utility room. If you need, add extra shelves so that you can keep things organized.

If you're worried about getting rid of documents with personal information on them, get a paper shredder or hire a shredding service to dispose of them for you.

Gather all of your product warranties and instruction manuals in one place (an expandable file can suit the purpose) to keep them organized and on-hand when needed.

When you're having difficulty deciding whether or not to get rid of an item, ask yourself these questions:
- Do I love it?
- Do I need it?
- Is it essential?
- Does it enhance my life?

Then, sort the items into the following three piles and deal with them accordingly:
- Yes — I love it and I need it, it works and it's useful so I'll keep it.
- No — Someone else can have it (either someone you know

or a charity).
• No — Put it in the garbage or recycling box.

Clearing out the clutter in your life
doesn't just get rid of old junk that gets in
the way, it also frees up your mind
and creates room for you to move forward
with important plans and goals.

25

INTEGRITY

As I write this I'm sitting in the New York Marriott Marquis Hotel following a 90-minute speech that I gave to the top U.S. book and magazine publishers. Watching TV in my room, I'm looking at the political life of the current New York governor, Eliot Spitzer, crumbling before my eyes. He has been accused of meeting with a prostitute in a Washington hotel.

Speaking to the question of why public figures such as Spitzer continue to get involved in these situations when they know that it will most likely lead to scandal and humiliation, Rabbi Brad Hirschfeld explains that, "It's about being bigger than the normal rules. The same thing that makes a person imagine they are big enough and bold enough to go be a CEO of a major company or the governor of the state of New York or the president of the United States is probably the same sense of grandeur that allows them to imagine they'll never get caught."

The governor resigned from his position on Wednesday, March 12, 2008, ending what New York state assemblyman John McEneny called, "one of the most promising careers I've seen in a generation."

It takes 20 years to build a reputation and five minutes to lose it. If you really think about that, you will choose to do things differently. You can lose money but you can't afford to lose your reputation. Most of my books and speeches deal with how to be successful. On the flip side, let's look at the five elements in life that, if we give in to them, are a direct path to failure sooner than later. They are:

1. Ego
2. Greed
3. Booze
4. Drugs
5. Illicit Sex

History books, newspapers and magazines are filled with people who indulged in these five elements and took high risks because they believed they alone controlled their fates or that their achievements — whether it be in the political arena, the corporate boardroom, onstage or the sports field — entitled them to break the rules and behave badly. More often than not, their stories end much like Mr. Spitzer's with the loss not only of a promising career but also the respect and admiration of their family, friends and the larger community.

The question we need to ask ourselves is, "How will what I say and do today affect my reputation and my life in the future and is it worth the risk?"

"A reputation once broken may possibly be repaired, but the world will always keep their eyes on the spot where the crack was."
— Joseph Hall

"The Lord judges the people; judge me, O Lord, according to my righteousness and according to the integrity that is in me."
— Psalm 7:8

26

DON'T IGNORE THE RULES

On a business trip to England, my daughter Rebecca and I found ourselves enjoying a meal in the oldest restaurant in London. Established in 1798, this venerable dining room is renowned not only for the food but also for the cavalcade of literary giants who, through the years, have made it their second home. Over the centuries it has been a favourite haunt of such legendary writers as Charles Dickens, William Makepeace Thackeray, John Galsworthy and H.G. Wells, as well as a comfortable respite of British royalty.

In the more than 200 years since it was founded, spanning the reigns of nine monarchs, this restaurant has been owned by only three families. Today it seats 200 guests on three floors, employs 100 staff and serves an average of 500 people a day — that's 150,000 customers a year.

Being curious types, we had to find out how this business has not only survived, but thrived. Edward Donnelly, the senior manager, agreed to share the secret of longevity and success of this fine old business. The restaurant, Donnelly told us, has only three rules — rules from which it never deviates.

> Rule One: Serve and specialize in a niche market — game meats.
> Rule Two: Take game meats seriously at all times.
> Rule Three: Adapt easily — no hierarchy.

These are the rules. And what is the name of the restaurant? You guessed it. It's called Rules! We, as business leaders, also need to have some basic rules to guide our path, but let's face it, nobody really likes rules. Thinking about that I came up with the idea of offering these guiding principles in booklet form and with that, my series titled *97 Tips* was born. To date, I have published three separate booklets that have been very well received. They are: *97 Tips on How to Deliver Great Customer Service*, *97 Tips on How to Jumpstart Your Career* and *97 Tips on How to Do Business in Tough Times*.

These back-to-basics tips booklets are a great Coles Notes for business leaders searching for ways to sharpen their focus and secure the profitability and long-term success of their enterprises. Running a small business, after all, is not rocket science. The key tenets of success invariably come back to simple basic principles. As Ralph Waldo Emerson said, "As to methods there may be a million and then some, but principles are few. The man who grasps principles can successfully select his own methods. The man who tries methods, ignoring principles, is sure to have trouble."

What guiding principles do you have for your business?

Have you written down your principles and communicated them to your employees and customers?

MAKING AN IMPACT

27

A MAGNIFICENT OBSESSION

I think it was Napoleon Hill who first came up with the concept of developing a "magnificent obsession" to help others, meaning that we should share our talents and resources with no expectation of a reward, payment or commendation, and above all else, keep our good turns a secret.

If you do this, you will set in motion the powers of a universal law. For, try as you will to avoid payment for your good deed, blessings and rewards will be showered upon you. I once heard someone say if you want to know what an individual is doing for their community, just look at what the community is doing for that individual. People who have given selflessly because they genuinely want to help others usually don't go unnoticed for very long.

My mentor Joe Segal is a good example. As a result of his outstanding contributions as a philanthropist, Joe has received numerous awards including both the Order of British Columbia and the Order of Canada; an Honorary Doctorate degree from Simon Fraser University, the Variety International Humanitarian Award (presented to both Joe and his wife Rosalie) and the Lions International Award of Merit, to name just a few. He has also been invested into the Venerable Order of St. John's of Jerusalem.

One of the reasons that I believe Joe is so generous is that he comes from humble beginnings and he understands what it means to work hard and to struggle. Joe Segal was born in a little town in Alberta called Vegreville, which is about halfway between Edmonton and Lloydminster.

Joe's father died when Joe was quite young — about 12 years old — so his beloved mother raised him alone. In his late teens, Joe got a job working on the Alaska Highway where there was no radio (this was the time before television), no newspapers and no magazines . . . just long hours of hard work.

So, Joe worked hard and saved up his money, some $3,500 in total by the time he headed back to Alberta (that was a small fortune back then). Arriving in Calgary at the Palliser Hotel, he hailed a cab and told the cabbie where he'd come from along with the fact that there were no newspapers, radio, magazines or other forms of entertainment.

With a look of amazement, the cabbie asked him, "So what did you do in your spare time?"

"Play poker," Joe replied.

The cabbie responded, "You fancy yourself a poker player. Do you want a game?"

"Sure," said Joe.

The cabbie took Joe to his hut where they played poker all night and when Joe came out of the game at dawn, he was flat broke — he had lost the entire $3,500.

With no money and nowhere to go, Joe decided that he would join the Navy. But when he arrived at the recruiting office, they told him he couldn't join up for a few weeks.

"I can't wait a few weeks. I need a job today!" Joe told them. So they sent him over to the Army recruiting office and he joined the Calgary Highlanders that very day.

Joe served his country in the Second World War and upon his return he decided to move to Vancouver. Hearing his plans, many people told Joe, "It's too big, you won't make it!"

"It's so big, I can't miss," Joe responded and off he went to Vancouver to seek his fortune.

Joe Segal was always an original — even then.

For his first big sales job, Joe found himself selling gallons of green war surplus paint and it was soon apparent that he was a very good salesman. For after Joe finished his route in the Fraser Valley, almost every barn in the region was painted army green.

With his natural sales ability, incredible people skills, the ability to do numbers in his head, a dedicated work ethic and a passion for business, Joe was well on his way along the road to success . . . but his world wasn't complete until Rosalie came into the picture. One look at Rosalie and Joe fell madly in love.

Unfortunately, Rosalie's father didn't approve. He once said of Joe, "He won't amount to anything!"

Obviously, Rosalie didn't agree. She and Joe have been married for more than 50 years. In that time, Joe built a retail empire that, at different times, included many names I am sure you're familiar with, such as Fields, Zellers (which, when it was bought by The Hudson Bay Company made Joe the largest shareholder), Mr. Jax, Sterling Shoes, Shoe Warehouse, Joneve Shoes; in addition to manufacturing companies and real estate investments.

Being a self-made man, over the years Joe's wisdom has been much sought after for all sorts of matters, particularly those related to business. In my book *The Runway of Life*, I told the story of a young man who, several years ago, sent Joe a note requesting an opportunity to meet with him and ask for advice — enclosed with the note was a $50 bill.

Being generous with his time, Joe would have met the young man without the $50 and upon meeting him, Joe returned the money. During their lunch, the young man posed his question to Joe, "How can I become wealthy without borrowing a lot of capital?"

"You can either go into real estate or the stock market," was Joe's advice. "You don't need capital for either of these careers. What you do need is a willingness for hard work, the ability to put in long hours and the discipline to learn the business."

The lunch ended and both men went their separate ways. However, some years later, the young man showed up at The Segal School of Business at Simon Fraser University, which is so named for the generous donation from Joe, Rosalie and their family to the beautiful heritage building (formerly the main branch of the Bank of Montreal on Granville Street) that houses the school in the heart of downtown Vancouver. Joe heard that the young man (now somewhat older) was visiting the Segal Graduate School and he decided to give him a personal tour of the facility, top to bottom, and find out how he had fared in the intervening years.

As they walked from floor to floor and room to room, Joe learned that the advice he had given the young man had paid off. He had gone into the stock market and was now a big success. Hearing that there were still a couple of classrooms that needed sponsorship money to complete renovations, the young man decided on the spot that he would give $200,000 to sponsor one of the rooms on the second floor as his way of saying thank you to Joe for taking the time to listen and offer some thoughtful advice years earlier.

Such is the life and generosity of the Segals who wish only to give back to the community they love. Joe asks for nothing.

As someone with a magnificent obsession to help others, Joe embodies the Jewish sage Hillel's words:

If I am not for myself, who will be for me?
If I am only for myself, who am I?
If not now, when?

Take a bold step, take action. Decide
now that you're going to be a person of
influence in your community.

As you Soar Higher in your own life,
look for ways to help others and develop a
magnificent obsession for contributing all that
you can to the community. Remember, the
world can always use one more hero.

28

WHO DARES WINS

Flying to London on British Airways in the spring of 2000, I found myself listening to an interview with someone from Britain's Special Air Service (SAS) on one of the inflight radio channels. In case you don't know, the SAS is an elite anti-terrorist unit that came into being in 1940 and since then has been deployed to almost every major conflict around the globe. As he summed up the philosophy of the SAS near the end of the interview, the fellow mentioned the organization's slogan, which is "Who Dares Wins." At the time I thought that it would make a great name for a book so I wrote it down.

Later, as I looked at the note again, I was reminded of all of the amazing people who, by their own example, have inspired me to challenge myself and continue to pursue ever-greater goals. I decided that this was a book that I had to write and that it would be an inspirational collection of stories about people who had succeeded in life by daring to go after their dreams. In writing it, I hoped that readers would gain insights that they could apply to both their professional endeavours and their personal journey in life.

Among the people featured in the book — both of whom I've had the pleasure of meeting — are Sir Edmund Hillary, whose historic climb up Mount Everest has inspired generations of individuals to push themselves to the limit; and astronaut Julie Payette, the first Canadian to board the International Space

Station and a role model for aspiring astronauts everywhere. The book also features many of my personal heroes, including Joe Segal, Grace McCarthy, Mel Cooper and Ray Addington, four people who have achieved legendary status in British Columbia, where I live.

What warms my heart as I look back on the books such as this one that I have written and the thousands of speeches that I have delivered over the years is just how much of an impact sharing these stories has had on the lives of others. Recently, former NHL hockey player Ryan Walter was a guest speaker at my church. As he walked into the building, Ryan turned to the pastor and asked, "Isn't this the church that Peter Legge goes to? I wonder if you could introduce him to me. He doesn't know this, but his career has had a great influence on me." Although Ryan and I have spoken on a few platforms together, I never thought he would think of me in those terms. It's very rewarding to know that.

Take some time today
to think about what you can do
in your own life to provide inspiration and
encouragement for others. Maybe it involves
taking on your very own Everest-sized
challenge, whatever that may be.

29

LIVE TOGETHER OR DIE ALONE

There is no doubt that we humans have achieved quite a lot since the world began. And much of what we have done is commend-able — a tribute to the smarts that come with being human. That's the good news. The bad news is that while we've been doing many things that we believe are for the betterment of all, these things are often done for selfish reasons. Too often we have waged wars, turned away from suffering and done far too much damage to the earth, wrongly believing that our planet has the capacity and resources to forever serve our wants and needs.

The good news (once again) is that in the nick of time we seem to be recognizing that some massive attitudinal corrections are in order. We can't keep waging wars and turning away from those in need and we *must* learn to live in closer harmony with the ecosystems that make Planet Earth the amazing life-sustain-ing place it is — or risk destroying it all.

I could be wrong, but I think that many more of us have become conscious of the fact that this sharing and giving has to happen if we want to look forward to a continuing, better world tomorrow. I also think that many of us are beginning to realize that the value of this planet can be counted in many more ways than those we might consider as simply economic. We're slowly learning to pay attention to the environment that surrounds us, to learn lessons from the beasts of the forest and the birds of the air. The wonders of the natural world are inspiring more of us to think anew about life, our dreams and our personal and social responsibilities.

Just as all of the characters on the popular TV show *Lost* (both the plane-crash survivors and the "others") eventually had to work together to fight to save the island, we too must find a way to work together to preserve the planet that is our island. As Jack's character on *Lost* so eloquently put it when the survivors began to break into factions and work at cross purposes to one another, "We can live together or die alone."

"Coming together is a beginning.
Keeping together is progress.
Working together is success."
— Henry Ford

30

AN AUSTRALIAN DEFINITION
OF A CANADIAN

You probably missed it in the local news, but there was a report that someone in Pakistan had advertised in a newspaper an offer of a reward to anyone who killed a Canadian — any Canadian. An Australian dentist wrote the following editorial to help define what a Canadian is, so they would know one when they found one:

A Canadian can be English, or French, or Italian, Irish, German, Spanish, Polish, Russian or Greek. A Canadian can be Mexican, African, Indian, Chinese, Japanese, Korean, Australian, Iranian, Asian, Arab, Pakistani or Afghan. A Canadian may also be a Cree, Métis, Mohawk, Blackfoot, Sioux or one of the many other tribes known as native Canadians. A Canadian's religious beliefs range from Christian, Jewish, Buddhist, Muslim, Hindu or none.

In fact, there are more Muslims in Canada than in Afghanistan. The key difference is that in Canada they are free to worship as each of them chooses. Whether they have a religion or no religion, each Canadian ultimately answers only to God, not to the government, or to armed thugs claiming to speak for the government and for God.

A Canadian lives in one of the most prosperous lands in the history of the world. The root of that prosperity can be found in the *Charter of Rights and Freedoms*, which recognizes the right of each person to the pursuit of happiness. A Canadian is generous and Canadians have helped out just about every other nation in the world in their time of need, never asking a thing in return. Canadians welcome the best of everything, the best products, the best books, the best music, the best food, the best services and the best minds. But they also welcome the least — the oppressed, the outcast and the rejected.

These are the people who built Canada. You can try to kill a Canadian if you must as other blood-thirsty tyrants in the world have tried, but in doing so, you could just be killing a relative or a neighbour. This is because Canadians are not a particular people from a particular place. They are the embodiment of the human spirit of freedom. Everyone who holds to that spirit, everywhere, can be a Canadian.

Canadians have helped out
just about every other nation in the
world in their time of need, never
asking a thing in return.

31

THE POWER TO SPEAK

Many years ago, as a young wannabe speaker, I ran into Earl Nightingale, considered at the time to be the Dean of Professional Speakers. He holds the distinction of having the very first million-copy seller — a spoken record called *The Magic Secret*.

When I asked for his advice, he told me, "Learn the art of being an excellent platform speaker and the doors of opportunity that will open for you will dwarf even your wildest dreams."

At the time, I thought that's easy for you to say, you're world renowned. I was just starting out. But I took his advice to heart and put all of my effort into becoming the best speaker I could be. Over the past 25 years, I've studied the many facets of the art of speaking and even though I feel that there is always something more to learn and opportunities for me to improve, I have been blessed to receive more awards for speaking than any other Canadian professional speaker. And the places I've gone as a result of my speaking career — including Buckingham Palace, Government House and The White House — would even have impressed Earl Nightingale.

The ability to speak well in public is an important one, even if you don't aspire to be the next Earl Nightingale. It is also something that strikes terror in the hearts of many. That's why most people at a funeral would rather be in the casket than giving the eulogy. It's also why they invented Toastmasters, which has literally thousands of clubs around the world and is a good place to start if you want to build your confidence and learn the basics of public speaking.

One of the primary reasons that I think I have been successful as a speaker is because I love to tell stories and always find something specific that allows me to connect with each audience. For example, I was speaking in Richmond, Virginia, for the first time at a conference with 800 delegates.

Knowing that Richmond is the birthplace of Patrick Henry, who is famous for his speech that includes the line, "Give me liberty or give me death," I took some time to visit a number of sites in this historic city. On the Saturday before my presentation, I visited St. Paul's Church, which is located downtown, and sat in the pew that Robert E. Lee and his family once occupied. I also visited St. John's Church, the site where Patrick Henry gave his speech and later that evening, committed the entire speech to memory.

The next day, I began my presentation by describing my visit to the various tourist attractions in the area and then segued into a recitation of the full text of Patrick Henry's speech. Although most people are familiar with the most famous line, few know the rest of the speech and so it was that a rather stunned audience sat and listened as a visiting Canadian delivered the entire speech with all the passion and conviction that Patrick Henry displayed as he urged Virginians to take up arms against the British in 1775.

Here is the final paragraph of Patrick Henry's speech:

"It is in vain, sir, to extenuate the matter. Gentlemen may cry, Peace, Peace — but there is no peace. The war is actually begun! The next gale that sweeps from the north will bring to our ears the clash of resounding arms! Our brethren are already in the field! Why stand we here idle? What is it that gentlemen wish? What would they have? Is life so dear, or peace so sweet, as to be purchased at the price of chains and slavery? Forbid it, Almighty God! I know not what course others may take; but as for me, give me liberty or give me death!"

Not surprisingly, the audience was attentive and engaged for the remainder of my 90-minute presentation and at the end I received a rousing standing ovation. By showing that I was interested in them and their history, I was able to create a special connection with my audience and deliver a memorable experience.

Always deliver more than you are paid to do and find a way to connect with your clients. Surprise them. Find out something that is important to them, that maybe they don't even know.

"There are three things to aim at in public speaking: first, to get into your subject, then to get your subject into yourself, and lastly, to get your subject into the heart of your audience."
— Alexander Gregg

32

THE HOW OF "WOW"

A while back, when my friend and fellow speaker Brian Tracy had just released a brand new book, *The Art of Closing Sales*, I decided to put on a one-week sales course for the team at Canada Wide Media. I bought a copy of the book for each of the guys and every morning for five days we sat down to talk about one chapter.

The session got started each morning at precisely 7:30 a.m. and it was mandatory for everyone on the sales team to participate. Working through the book together, the week was very productive. To show my appreciation for their hard work, at the end of session on Friday, I had prepared to give each of the sales staff a graduation certificate from the "Peter Legge School of Sales." But I also wanted to add a "wow" factor to the experience to make it truly memorable, so I got in touch with my good friend Brian Tracy who was conducting one of his seminars in Boston and I asked him if he would phone our boardroom at exactly 8:30 a.m. on the Friday.

When the call from Brian came in right on cue, my sales guys were suitably impressed and as Brian did a 10-minute motivational message live on the phone about his book and about selling, I could see that they were hanging on his every word. It was exactly what was needed to get them pumped up and ready to put what they had learned into action and I knew that it would be something they would remember for a long time. I could also tell by the looks on their faces when the call was over that most of them were thinking, "How the hell did he get Brian Tracy to phone at exactly 8:30 while he was handing out those certificates?"

The answer to that question is simple and it's something that I talk about elsewhere in this book. I could do it because of the strong relationships that I have built up during my years of business. It is exactly the kind of relationship that I was asking my sales team to build with our customers. Because of my long-standing friendship with Brian Tracy as a fellow speaker, I knew that when I called to ask this favour, if he was able, he would willingly oblige, in the same way that I obliged when I was asked to introduce him at the Ford Theatre this past February when he did his presentation in Vancouver.

What can you do to produce a "wow" factor for the people that you influence and motivate? Look for opportunities to make experiences memorable.

33

THE SECRET

In British Columbia, the long weekend in May generally signals the beginning of summer. In the metro Vancouver area, people leave early from work on a Friday to beat the traffic as they head to popular warm spots such as the Okanagan; the golf courses are full, the highways and byways around the province are overflowing with people towing holiday trailers and boats; the BC Ferries are oversold as people head to the islands for a bit of R&R.

Generally, I'm as caught up in celebrating the first long weekend of the season as anyone, but this year was different. The day before the long weekend began I received an unexpected telephone call from Karen Felker, who is with the Honours and Awards Secretariat for the province of British Columbia. Karen was calling to let me know that the advisory council for the Order of B.C. had recommended my appointment to the Order.

Was I excited?

You bet!

Did I want to call every single person I know to give them the news?

Absolutely!

The problem was that because it still had to be approved by Cabinet, Karen advised me that I was only to tell my wife and children — no one else. I guess if someone had wanted to test my ability to keep a secret, this would have been an excellent way to do it because it was the better part of a month before the province announced the Order recipients to the public and for me, it was like sitting on pins and needles.

As the highest civilian honour that you can get in this province, I am extremely grateful to receive The Order of B.C. and I know that my parents would have been so proud of me, as my wife and children are. With all of the love, support and encouragement they have given me, I like to think that the award is as much for all of them as it is for me. It's also a testament to all of the great organizations that have allowed me to assist them in some way. I'm indebted to them all for this privilege. It's amazing what you can accomplish if you keep doing good things.

Not sure who to help? Phone your local charity and ask for the executive director. Offer some of your time, energy and talent, and maybe some money. Your life will be richer for doing so.

I want to take this opportunity to say thank you to all of the people who have contributed to my success — in business and in the community. No one succeeds alone.

ATTITUDE IS EVERYTHING

34

BIG LESSONS CAN HAPPEN EVEN IN THE SMALLEST OF PLACES

I hold a special place in my heart for the Williams Lake Cattlemen's Association. Not because of any particular love of cattle, or for that matter, of any particular individuals within the association, but because the Williams Lake Cattlemen's Association taught me a very important lesson about life.

In the course of my speaking career, I have jetted in the best of seats to speak in some amazing international venues. Many of these engagements took place in spectacular world destinations, where I found myself checked into luxurious rooms and served the finest food and wine. As a result, I have shared conversations with some of the most talented, successful and inspiring people you could ever dream of meeting. To borrow an overused phrase, it's been world-class stuff.

On one such occasion I was scheduled to speak in Vienna and my hosts had spared no expense, arranging to fly my wife and myself to Austria first class and provide a suite with all the bells and whistles. Just before I left for Austria I received a call asking me if I would speak at the annual meeting of the Cattlemen's Association in the small town of Williams Lake, B.C.

I asked the booking agent if they would be flying me up in a jet.

"Certainly," she responded.

"Are they picking me up in a limo?" I inquired.

"Of course," she assured me.

"Will I be speaking at the convention centre?"

"Absolutely!"

"Do they have a state-of-the-art sound system?"

"Most assuredly!"

Feeling satisfied, I accepted the engagement.

As it turned out, the private jet was a Dash 8 that stopped in three different places on its journey between Vancouver and Williams Lake. When I arrived at the airport, there was no one waiting at the gate to greet me and as the small terminal quickly cleared and I walked outside, it was obvious that there was to be no limo either. The only vehicle in sight was a dusty yellow mini bus idling at the front curb.

"I'm expecting a limo," I told the driver who was waiting beside the bus.

"You must be Mr. Legge," he said smiling. "Hop in, this is your limousine."

I took a seat and we bumped along into town, but instead of arriving at the convention centre as I had expected, the bus pulled up in front of the local arena. Apparently, this was to be my speaking venue. I walked inside to find that the arena floor had been set up with a makeshift stage and chairs arranged in rows for the audience. The state-of-the-art sound system I had been promised turned out to be the microphone that the announcer had used for the hockey game the night before and the whole place was stale, dank and dusty.

I was not a happy camper. After all, I was used to much better than this.

It wasn't until I walked into the washroom and caught a glimpse of myself in the mirror that I realized the truth of the situation. As I stood there sulking and feeling sorry for myself, what I saw reflected back at me was the face of a spoiled, petulant brat.

"Who are you to demand limousines and fancy venues?" I asked my reflection. "These people are as honest, genuine and welcoming as anyone you have encountered, maybe even more so, and they have provided you with the best that they have to offer."

Realizing that if I carried on in this manner it would be me who was not living up to the terms of our agreement — not the good people of Williams Lake — I snapped myself into shape, wiped the dust from my shoes, straightened my tie, combed my hair, added a big smile and went out there to give them my very best.

Looking back, I don't think that I have ever made a more inspired and genuine presentation than I did that day. What I remember most is the standing ovation they gave me. I also remember the warmth of those people who made their living from the land and showed me with their smiles and their handshakes that they appreciated what I had to offer.

After I had said my goodbyes, I rode back to the airport in the same bus that had brought me to the arena with the very same driver, but this time, my attitude was safely stored in my luggage, along with an important lesson that I have remembered to this day.

I flew back from Williams Lake that evening with a feeling of exhilaration, of wanting to return to tell those weathered and wonderful cattlemen that they had done me a great favour — because they did. They taught me an important life lesson *and* gave me a great story.

Today, I often tell my audiences that you just never know when something wonderful is going to hit you right between the eyes and it can happen anywhere — big places, small places, even when you are standing alone in front of the mirror in a dusty washroom in Williams Lake.

Had I not straightened out my attitude on that day, I would have missed one of the best speaking engagements of that season. As a result, I learned not to let my own expectations get in the way of doing my job to the best of my abilities. I also learned that while fancy jets and limousines are nice, they've got nothing on genuine hospitality.

Don't let your expectations — or your ego — get in the way of treating everyone you meet with the respect they deserve and doing your job to the very best of your abilities.

35

EXERCISE YOUR ENTHUSIASM

Enthusiasm is one of the most desirable of human qualities. Not only does it attract people to you, but it also causes them to want to cooperate with you and help in any way possible. Enthusiasm is the spark that touches off the dormant power housed in your brain and puts it into action. It is also a sure antidote for laziness or procrastination and it is the main spring that keeps your mental machinery in action.

Enthusiasm overcomes despondency and generates hope, self-confidence and courage. It even stirs up your liver and puts it to work, thereby helping it carry on its vital function of cleansing your blood. Enthusiasm arouses your whole being and causes you to transform your dreams into reality!

If you find that you're not enthusiastic about your work (or any other aspect of your life), the obvious reason is that you don't really love what you're doing and you owe it to yourself and others to make a change to something that is better suited to your interests and talents — and something you *can* be enthusiastic about.

Enthusiasm is contagious. When you're excited and motivated, you unconsciously pass it on to those with whom you come into contact and it arouses them to act and think as you do. An enthusiastic person, when guided by a sense of justice toward others, is a great asset in any organization, business, family or community.

According to Charles C. Krulak, a General in the U.S. Marine Corps, who wrote about *The Fourteen Basic Traits of Effective Leadership,* "Enthusiasm is a trait easily identifiable in successful leaders in all walks of life. It is easy to infuse energy when you exude energy. Enthusiasm is more than just attitude, however. It permeates the work at hand. Routine lectures become interesting presentations and tedious projects become intriguing endeavours. Enthusiasm is contagious — and doubly so when it originates from a figure whom people respect."

Are you a person of enthusiasm?

36

HOW HUNGRY ARE YOU?

Ryan Walter played more than 1,000 games over 15 seasons in the NHL during his hockey career. He was captain of the Washington Capitals. He played nine seasons with the Montreal Canadiens and won a Stanley Cup during his tenure. He finished his career in his hometown of Vancouver as assistant captain of the Vancouver Canucks.

Born in Burnaby, B.C., Ryan is now a much sought-after motivational speaker and leadership coach. Recently, he spoke at my church and one of the key questions that he asked the members of the congregation was, "Are you hungry?"

According to Ryan, the difference between first place and second place is not about talent and it's not about coaching, it's about being hungry enough to go out and do what it takes to get the job done, whether it's scoring goals, scoring new accounts or scoring a promotion.

The opposite of hungry isn't "not hungry"; it's ambivalence, which really means, "I don't care." Take that attitude on a hockey team and it won't be long before you find yourself out of a job. Take that attitude in life and chances are you won't get very far either. Why? Because in the same way that hockey championships are won by the teams that are generally the most hungry, so too is the business world dominated by those companies that are willing to deliver above and beyond what their competition does. And the people who are most successful in life? They're the ones who want it so bad that they can actually taste it.

How hungry are you to achieve your dreams; your goals in life; the vision you have for your company, your career, your family, your community?

Stay hungry and see what happens!

37

IT'S ALL IN YOUR HEAD

I was listening to John Tesh on Clear FM Radio one morning while I was driving to a meeting and I heard him do an interview where he was talking about long-distance runners. What caught my attention about the topic was a comment that he made about how the fatigue that these athletes experience when they "hit the wall" is more of a mental thing and not a physical phenomenon.

That interview got me thinking about how much of who we "are" is all in our head. Personally, I think that every day is full of opportunity and it fills me with tremendous energy. That's why it surprises me when someone half my age comes into my office in the morning and says, "I'm exhausted" after a presumably pretty good night's sleep. I don't understand.

It's important to remember that our brain doesn't know what's real or otherwise; it's our thinking that makes it so. If you think you're tired, that's the way that your body is going to respond. Just like if you think that you're successful or if you think that you're happy, that's what you'll be. It's powerful stuff.

"You become what you think about most of the time." I got that quote from Earl Nightingale. Ralph Waldo Emerson also said something like it, as did Shakespeare. It's one of those enduring bits of wisdom that many of the great thinkers through the ages have touched on.

The power to be or to do anything is really all in our head.

"There is nothing either good or bad, but thinking makes it so," that's from Hamlet.

"As you think in your heart, so shall you be," the wise words of King Solomon.

Unfortunately, it's an age-old wisdom that we sometimes forget. I find the best way to remember important truisms like this one is to write them down, look at them often and use them when I am planning and setting my goals — I also put them in my books to share with others.

Does your thinking support what you truly want in your life, do you "think" that you are successful, happy and healthy?

How could you "think" better to be better?

38

FREE ATTITUDE ADJUSTMENT
WITH EVERY SHINE

I was in St. Louis for a speaking engagement when I happened across a little place called Shed Shoe Shine. On the lapel of the fellow working there was a nametag with the word "SHED" printed on it. This got me curious, so I asked him, "Is that your real name? Is that your nickname? Who on earth would name a guy Shed?" Hearing my barrage of questions, the fellow wheeled back and said, "No, my name is Shed, my mama named me Shed and that's who I am."

In addition to the unusual nametag, he also had a stethoscope around his neck so I asked what it was for. He told me, "I've been shining shoes for 35 years and some people call me the doctor of shining shoes." To which he added, "Some people also call me the saviour of soles."

As I looked around, I noticed a sign on his shoeshine stand that said, "If you've got a good attitude, I charge you two dollars, if you've got a bad attitude, I charge you six dollars," and I asked him "How so?" He said, "Because it costs you to have a bad attitude. It costs with your spouse, it costs with your children, it costs with your neighbours, it costs with the people you work with and it certainly costs with your customers when you have a bad attitude."

That night at my presentation, I told the story of my encounter with Shed and the next morning there were 15 men lined up to get their shoes shined with Shed. Somehow, I don't think they were just there because their shoes were scuffed, I really suspect that they wanted their attitudes adjusted along with the shine.

Attitude is everything. You can take two companies that provide virtually the same kind of service at a similar cost, or you can take two speakers for the same fee and similar content, or even two shoeshine guys with similar skills and experience, but the individual with the most infectious, positive attitude will always win out . . . always.

I'm glad I met Shed and I'm glad each of us was able to help the other. I got a story and he got some new customers.

Have you checked your attitude lately? How does it affect the people around you?

Would you need a $2 or a $6 shine?

39

LEARN TO LOVE CHANGE

In the Bible, it states 323 times, "This too shall pass." Nowhere does it say, "This will stay." Buddhists, too, have a word to describe the state of impermanence that applies to all things. They call it anicca. The following story illustrates how our attitude towards change can determine the happiness we experience in life.

A rich old man died leaving behind two sons. As they did not want to live together, they decided to divide all the properties between themselves, 50-50. However, just as all matters related to the property were settled, the two brothers came across a small packet carefully hidden by their father. The packet contained two rings; one was an expensive diamond ring and the other an ordinary silver ring, worth only a few dollars at most.

Seeing the diamond ring, the elder brother desired to have it for himself. He explained to the younger brother, "This packet is obviously a family heirloom and not part of the joint family property, our father evidently desired the diamond ring to be passed on from generation to generation and stay within the family. Therefore, being the elder brother I will take the diamond ring. You had better take the silver one."

The younger brother smiled and agreed.

Yet the younger brother was curious as to why the father

had preserved the silver ring, which obviously had very little value. He took out the ring and examined it. On the ring were written four words, "This too will pass." "Aahh, now I understand," the younger brother said to himself. "This was the motto of my father and the ring served as a reminder." He placed the ring on his finger.

Time passed and both brothers went through the usual ups and downs of life. The elder brother was always happy when spring came and he was prosperous for he had developed a strong attachment to material things. However, when winter approached and times were leaner he always became highly anxious. He needed medication and sleeping pills to be able to sleep. When that did not help, he completely lost his balance and needed visits to the psychiatrist and electric shock treatments. This was the brother with the diamond ring.

The younger brother also enjoyed the springtime when it came, but remembered his father's motto — this too will change. He did not get attached to his circumstances but enjoyed them while they lasted. When spring passed he said to himself, "It was inevitable that it would pass and now it has done so. So what?" Similarly, when winter approached and circumstances turned harsh, he did not become agitated but remembered, this too will pass. Thus he was able to preserve his sense of balance through all the ups and downs of life and lived with a sense of happiness and fulfillment.

Which ring have you chosen to wear?

If we stop to think about it, everything in the world is continually changing — and not even one of us is the same person we were 20 years ago. All of the cells in our body, our appearance, our personality, our feelings and emotions, even our problems have changed in that time. Good or bad, with time, everything changes.

With change come challenges.

Most things that seem insurmountable can be managed if you simply choose to face up to the situation at hand. Start by asking yourself, "Given my choices, what is the worst that can happen with each potential action? And what will likely happen if I take no action at all?" Decide what action you can take to get through the situation and break it down step-by-step if necessary. If you need to make something right, do so. If you need to confront a situation, take care of it. If you need to grieve, do that and then move on.

Have you learned to welcome the changes that life inevitably brings?

40

TO HAVE AND HAVE NOT

There is a legend I read recently about a Burmese potter who had become envious of the prosperity of a washerman. Determined to put this man out of business, the potter convinced the king to issue an order requiring the man to wash one of the emperor's black elephants and make it white. The washerman replied that according to the rules of his vocation, he would need a vessel large enough to hold the elephant, whereupon the king commanded the potter to provide one.

So the potter constructed a giant bowl and had it carefully delivered to the washerman. But when the elephant stepped into it, it crumbled to pieces beneath the weight of the enormous beast. Many more vessels were made, but each was crushed in the same way. Eventually it was the potter who was put out of business by the very same scheme he had devised to ruin the man he envied.

Although the world is a competitive place, being envious of what others have or spending time trying to undermine the success of a competitor can only lead to disaster in the end, if for no other reason than it will poison the sweet taste that comes from an honest victory or the satisfaction of knowing — win or lose — that you did your best.

Be grateful to your competitors
for challenging you to push yourself further
and accomplish more.

You cannot control what others do
— only what you can do.

41

EVEN IN NEW YORK

My expectations were high. I had a speaking engagement in New York City, the Big Apple. Frank Sinatra's big hit, *New York, New York* was ringing in my head, particularly the line, "If you can make it there, you'll make it anywhere."

My wife Kay had joined me for the trip and one of our daughters, Rebecca, was flying in from Toronto for the weekend. So, as I said, expectations were high and I had done my homework. My presentation was written and I was familiar with the audience, the only thing left was to do a pre-performance check of the theatre where I would be speaking.

We flew from Vancouver to New York's John F. Kennedy airport on Cathay Pacific, arguably one of the highest-rated airlines in the world. Halfway through the five-hour flight, I asked one of the flight attendants, whose name was Jim, "How long did you train for this job?"

"Almost four months," he replied.

Then I asked, "What one element other than passenger safety really stuck with you from your training?"

Without missing a beat he answered, "Attention to detail."

It was a great sign to begin my trip.

For me, New York is all about Broadway shows, glitz, glamour . . . the good life. And here we were staying at a hotel overlooking Times Square, the show business capital of the world where everything is done world class. As I arrived at the conference for my speaking engagement, I was expecting the very best in technical, AV and lighting in the aptly titled "Broadway Ballroom" where I would be speaking.

I showed up at my usual 90 minutes prior to show time to conduct a sound check, rehearse my AV requirements and check on the lighting, room set-up and heating. To my amazement, there were no lights on the platform — which meant that the audience wouldn't be able to see my face while I was speaking to them. The room, a cavernous ballroom, was set up for 200 attendees but could have easily accommodated 1,500.

Following what can only be described as a very poor introduction, I began my speech and I can tell you it's really tough to connect with 200 people scattered around in such a huge venue. Adding to the difficulty of a large space, the doors at the back of the room had been left open allowing noise from outside to filter into the room and distract the audience. When it was time to play my Olympic DVD, there was sound, but no picture on the screen and during the last four minutes of my presentation, a latecomer showed up, walked the entire length of the theatre and sat himself down in the front row.

As I finished my presentation and stood waiting at the podium, a conference facilitator came on stage and without a thank you or any other acknowledgement of my presence, encouraged the people to move on to the breakout sessions (there weren't even any evaluation forms).

At this, a chap sitting in the front row (not the latecomer, incidentally) looked around in bewilderment and said, "Is that it?"

That was my question too. I was flabbergasted, mostly because the majority of conference organizers that I have worked with go out of their way to make the venue "work" for the speaker and to facilitate the success of their presentation.

As an organizer myself, I remember one time that we had the

comedian Bob Hope do one of our events and in front of the stage there was a dance floor so the seats had been set around that. Prior to the event, Bob came in to have a look at the set-up and do his sound check. He took one look at the empty space in front of the stage, which was a polished wood floor, turned to me and said, "Peter, wood doesn't laugh. Fill it in," and walked out of the room.

As organizers, we scrambled, along with the hotel staff to move tables and chairs right up to the stage so he could be more intimate with the audience, something that all speakers strive for.

You could say that my New York trip didn't go exactly as planned, but it hasn't in any way changed my affection for the city or for speaking at conferences. I still love both and experience has taught me how to deal with such situations gracefully. No matter what we do in life, no matter what goes wrong, we need to be as professional as we can be. Not everything goes the way we expect it to and we have to rise above it for that hour, or that day or that week. Not everything is perfect, not even in New York City.

Life is far from perfect, but learning to accept its imperfections with grace can go a long way towards a smoother, happier life.

42

THE GOOD LIFE

It's a real pleasure to get away to our condo in Palm Springs whenever we can. For me, it is a time to reflect, think, strategize, write and lay plans for the future. In mid-January of this past year, my wife Kay and I were doing just that when, intertwined with a few rounds of golf, the idea of this book came about.

What got me started was thinking about just how good we've got it here in the 21st century. You see, my birthday is on January 14 (which keeps coming around every year whether I want it to or not) and one of my presents this time was a book titled *Augustus: The Life of Rome's First Emperor* by Anthony Everitt.

The first paragraph of the second chapter in the book really jumped out at me. *"The year 49 B.C. saw the world turned upside down. The Roman Republic was facing catastrophe, thanks to a civil war."*

What were the causes of this crisis, I wondered. Stubborn political, military and economic facts, coupled with the antics of colourful but obstinate personalities. Sounds a bit like today in our world with the United States on the verge of recession, the ongoing war in Iraq and everyone worried about the rising price of oil. Everyone is thinking doom and gloom these days and many people are pointing fingers at American president George W. Bush. Yet, compared to what the world was like even a hundred years ago, we have absolutely no problems today, we live in a world with freedom, technology, convenience and opportunity.

Chapter Two went on . . . *"It was also the inadvertent outcome of astonishing success."*

Napoleon Hill said, "Every adversity, every failure and every heartache carries with it the seed of an equivalent or greater benefit."

There's also the old saying about necessity being the mother of invention. I agree. It's important to use the opportunity that is provided by those things that we are dissatisfied with to make our world better. Rather than simply complaining about high gas prices, why not do something about it? After all, we have all of the resources at hand to innovate and develop new methods of fuel conservation and alternative energy sources. Likewise, if we're unhappy with the current direction that politicians are taking the world in, in most developed countries at least, we have constitutional protection that allows us to get involved in the political process, join with other likeminded individuals and make sure our voice is heard — and the Internet is a great equalizer in this regard, offering virtually anyone with a computer the ability to reach out and broadcast their message to the world. We also have the freedom to work in any profession we choose, to own property, start a business or come up with the next "big" idea like Google, HD (high definition) technology or virtual reality. We truly are living the good life.

The only question you have to ask yourself now is, "What am I going to do today to make the most of the opportunities that lie before me and the potential within me?"

43

WICKED

"Within you right now is the power
to do things you never dreamed possible.
This power becomes available
to you just as soon as you can change
your beliefs."
— Maxwell Maltz

I took two of my daughters to see the play *Wicked* in New York City recently at the Gershwin Theatre on 52nd Street. A musical, *Wicked* is like a prequel to *The Wizard of Oz* and tells the story of how Glinda the Good Witch and the Wicked Witch of the West were once friends, in the time before Dorothy came to Oz.

In the play, the Wicked Witch of the West has supernatural powers that any human would love to have. Given her powers, what struck me as odd is that halfway through the play, the Wicked Witch says to Glinda, "I have limitations." From where I was sitting, it didn't look to me as if she had any limitations, but afterwards I got to thinking that although other people might not be able see them, we all have limitations — even if they are simply the ones that we have put on ourselves.

Limitations aren't real; they are something that the mind conjures to deal with fear. In reality you have no limitations. You can do anything if you make up your mind to do it because determination always finds a way around obstacles. Do you remember Henry Ford's words? "If you think you can . . . or if you think you can't . . . you're right." It all depends on what you believe about yourself.

It's often been said that what you believe becomes your reality. Meaning that you don't believe what you see; rather, you will see what you already believe. That's why two people facing the exact same situation or set of circumstances may interpret it differently and take different actions based on their beliefs, which results in two different outcomes.

When you have self-limiting beliefs, it is like stepping on the brakes in your car and expecting the car to move forward. More often than not, our limitations come from a distorted perspective of the world around us. We look at other people and we see all that they *have*, then we look at ourselves and we only see what we *don't* have or we carry on into adulthood with negative programming that we picked up in our earlier years when we experienced criticism, embarrassment or failure.

Fortunately, you can rid yourself of self-limiting beliefs, but to do so you have to identify what they are. Often, these thoughts and beliefs lurk in the background without us being consciously aware of them. Talking with a friend or colleague or consulting with a coach or mentor could provide you with more objective feedback as to which beliefs are getting in the way of your success.

Once you have identified them, these limiting beliefs must be challenged every time they come up in your mind. One way to do this is to consciously replace your thoughts about limitations with mental or verbal affirmations such as, "I can accomplish anything I set my mind to," or "There are no limitations to what I can achieve."

Attacking these self-limiting thoughts and replacing them with positive ones is like pulling the weeds from your garden so that you can plant fruits and vegetables that will provide you with food. As Jim Rohn advises, "You cannot take the mild approach to the weeds in your mental garden. You have got to hate weeds enough to kill them. Weeds are not something you handle; weeds are something you devastate."

Never underestimate the power of your own thoughts to determine the direction of your life. Choose to nurture only those that enhance your perception of what is possible and help you to achieve your goals.

Three Tips to Keep You on the Right Track:
Aim for something.
If you want to get past your limitations, you need to aim toward a specific target. Set realistic goals or even mini goals that will take you step by step towards a larger goal. For example, if you're out of shape because you "never have time for exercise," start getting up 30 minutes earlier to make time and rather than telling yourself that you need to get in shape because you're 30 pounds overweight, talk about how you are doing it to increase your energy and get healthier. Positive goals provide more powerful motivation than negative ones. As you make small improvements, continue to raise the target.

Keep your focus.
With our busy lives, it's not unusual for our attention to be

dispersed in many different directions at once with the result that our energy is equally dispersed, something that makes us both less effective and more vulnerable to backsliding. Take the time to concentrate and focus on what you want to accomplish and you'll find that results become much more spontaneous.

Don't listen to other people's negativity.
Although critics are great if you want the lowdown on a new movie or play, they're not so great at providing the motivation you need to be successful. It's important to be able to tell the difference between constructive advice and criticism. Progress doesn't come from listening to the doubts, suspicions and disbelief of others. When you can learn to ignore negativity — from yourself and others — you will truly be free to Soar Higher.

Never underestimate the power of your own thoughts to determine the direction of your life.

SERVICE MATTERS

44

IT'S ALL ABOUT SERVICE

Some years ago, during a visit to London, England, some friends and I decided to drive through the famed Chunnel and visit Paris for dinner. Upon arriving in the City of Light, we indulged ourselves in the meal of a lifetime at a fine restaurant only to discover at the end of the meal that the restaurant did not take credit cards of any kind.

With only enough francs between us to cover a small tip, never mind the cost of the meal, we were panic stricken. When I explained our dilemma to the manager, he calmly asked for my business card and, satisfied that I was completely on the level, told me that he would present me with an invoice to be paid within 30 days. I was completely flabbergasted — and immensely relieved.

The manager took a calculated risk — one that resulted in this story being retold in my first book and to audiences on more than a hundred occasions since. To this day, I still tell everyone I know that when they visit Paris, they should make a point to visit Lasserre Restaurant at 17 Avenue Franklin-Roosevelt, 75008 Paris.

The moral of the story: every time you interact with a customer, whether you are the clerk in a small convenience store or the manager of a fancy restaurant, you have an opportunity to make or break the experience for your customer. So give the best service you know how to render, regardless of the amount you receive for it, and soon — much sooner than you might imagine — you will become a "marked" person and greater responsibilities and higher wages will be thrusting themselves upon you.

Deliver the best services you can, not necessarily out of consideration for the purchaser but out of consideration for yourself! Failure to practice this habit is the chief obstacle that stands between 95 per cent of people and success, but of course this does not apply to you.

Or does it?

In a time when there is a shortage of workers, particularly in the retail sector and service industries, many staff and the companies they work for feel that this is an opportunity to skimp on service — it isn't. People want to do business with people they like and nobody enjoys being ignored, brushed off, talked down to or insulted.

Here are some ideas to help you improve the experience you provide for your customers:

Be the customer.
Customers are who we are when we are not working. Take the time to see your company as your customers do. Try standing on the other side of the counter and evaluate how you feel about the service you receive, or better yet, hire a few "secret shoppers" and have them provide a detailed report of how they experienced the service provided by your company. By walking around in their shoes for a while, you will have a much better understanding of your customer's perspective and be better able to both anticipate and meet their needs.

Engage your customers.

It's not always easy to ask for a critical opinion, but without your customers you wouldn't be in business at all. That's why it's important to engage your customers in a conversation about how they view your company. Why do they give you their business, what do they like about your company, what don't they like, would they recommend you to a friend or family member, and why or why not? Asking these sorts of questions on a regular basis, or offering some sort of reward to customers for providing their honest feedback, will help you gather valuable information on whether your customers are getting a great experience from your company. If you listen carefully, most customers will tell you what they want or need.

Never leave a complaint unanswered.

Many large companies simply ignore complaints received by email in the hope that the problem will go away. Imagine if you had a problem, how it would feel to be ignored in this way. Rather than thinking about it as a negative, approach every complaint as an opportunity to satisfy a customer who has already invested in the relationship by giving you their business.

Reward staff for great customer service.

Rewarding employees for good customer service is an excellent way to ensure that it continues to happen. We all work better when we have incentives, so take the time to reinforce good customer service by acknowledging it when it happens and rewarding staff with public recognition (an award or appreciation event), a financial bonus or a gift.

Failure to deliver the best service they can is the chief obstacle that stands between 95 per cent of people and success.

45

I'LL BE BACK

One of the magazines we publish at Canada Wide Media is for the BC Restaurant Association, which has 7,000 member restaurants throughout British Columbia and is a leading association for the industry. Much of what the magazine focuses on is helping restaurants to thrive in a very competitive marketplace where you can be the toast of the town one month and out of business the next.

Thinking about how they strive to serve the needs of their 7,000 members with industry news, the latest culinary trends and topical features, got me thinking that in the hospitality industry, the most important three words you want to hear from a customer are, "I'll be back."

A happy customer is a return customer and for the hospitality industry, along with every other business that serves the needs of customers (which is virtually every business), it all comes down to service. So, how do you get your customers to say those three little words? Easy, by following these three little words of advice, "Always be helpful."

Consider the following scenario: you've just arrived at your hotel after a long flight and checked into your hotel room. You're unpacking your bag and looking forward to a nice relaxing bath when you realize that you've forgotten an important medication at home. You immediately call the front desk because you need to find a pharmacy that can replace the medication before the end of the day. The clerk at the front desk answers the phone and asks how she can help you and you mention that you have a problem.

"OK," she replies, in a flat tone of voice.

Suddenly, you feel as if you've interrupted her. Her voice sounds distant, as if her attention is still on whatever it is that you've taken her away from, and although she hasn't overtly insulted you or said she's unwilling or unable to help, that's exactly the impression you get from her reply. With a simple, neutral word, she makes you feel inconsequential and uncomfortable.

"This shouldn't happen, should it?" says Dr. Gary S. Goodman, president of Customersatisfaction.com. "But it does, hundreds of thousands, if not millions of times a day. Careless employees that are allowed to casually script their own conversations alienate customers without knowing it, and their trainers, monitors and managers don't detect their flaws."

"There is a better way," says Dr. Goodman, whose solution is a simple one that ensures all customer service staff let the customer know that they are ready, willing and able to help. After a client mentions what they want, or asks a question, every staff member is simply trained to say, "Sure, I'll be happy to help you with that."

Imagine hearing that when you call the phone company to sort out a problem with your cell-phone bill or at the airline counter when your luggage is missing or the meal you ordered is awful and you have to send it back to the kitchen. It sends a clear signal that the employee is not only competent, but they are poised, prepared and eager to solve your problem. It says, "You're going to get the service you need and I'm going to enjoy providing it for you."

Are you communicating the promise of help to your customers?

It's important not to assume that your staff members know your expectations of how they are to deliver service to your customers. If you want your staff to say, "Sure, I'll be happy to help you with that," communicate your expectations and make it an explicit part of their training. Also, put your expectations down on paper, review them regularly and make sure that all new staff members are properly trained too.

Why not try this approach in your business and see if you don't have more customers telling you, "I'll be back."

Here are a few more tips:

Take time with your customers.
People are coming to you to help them solve a problem or fill a need. Don't rush them. Often they will be happy to pay more for goods or services from a business that is willing to give them more time.

Don't let your customers leave dissatisfied.
There is no limit to the negative effect an unhappy customer can have on your business. A typical dissatisfied customer will tell eight to 10 people about their problem. One in five will tell 20 people. Even if you can't solve a customer's problem, you can still provide service, attention and offer recommendations to help find a solution. In this way, even if they never give you their business, at least they will have nice things to say about you to others.

Look after the little details.
Little things mean a lot. The Eaton's store that used to be in downtown Vancouver claimed to be "Canada's Department

Store," yet they regularly piped in music from an FM station in Seattle. As a customer I noticed. What little details are your customers paying attention to?

Speaking of great customer service and attention to detail, for those of you who like to travel and dine out, here are 10 of the best restaurants I've visited:
1. Rules — London, England
2. LG's Steakhouse — Palm Desert, California
3. Carnegie Deli — New York City
4. Barbarians — Toronto, Ontario
5. Mani Lani — Maui
6. Carver's Steakhouse — Saskatoon, Saskatchewan
7. T.G.I. Friday's — Washington, D.C. (invented potato skins)
8. Il Giardino — Vancouver, B.C.
9. Lasserre Restaurant — Paris, France
10. Ruth's Chris Steakhouse — Los Angeles (20 years)

There is no limit to the negative effect an unhappy customer can have on your business.

46

AND THEN SOME

As I mentioned in my book *The Runway of Life*, which was inspired by my mentor Joe Segal, I first met Joe in a small office in the back of a Fields store on West Hastings Street about 45 years ago. I was selling airtime for CJOR Radio in Vancouver back then and trying hard to make Joe one of my advertising clients.

In all the times that I called on him, Joe never bought any radio time and I guess if I weren't so thick headed, I'd have stopped calling on him after a while. But there was something about his mannerisms, his charm, his tactfulness and his sense of humour that kept me coming back.

Although we drifted our separate ways for a few years after I moved onto another job, Joe never forgot me. Joe never forgets anyone. A decade or so went by and we came back into each other's lives — Joe, a monumental success and me just starting out with my own business. It was 1976 and I asked Joe for his advice on how to make my business grow.

"Too many times in life, we see a need but hesitate to act on it," Joe told me. "Believe it or not, the best opportunities don't come in a package with a bow. In fact, more often than not they present themselves in the form of a problem. Successful people are those who are willing to put their neck on the line and take a risk — they see a need and act decisively to find a way to fulfill it."

Great advice.

Retired business executive Carl Holmes was once asked the secret of his success. This is what he had to say:

"And then some . . . these three little words are the secret of success.

They are the difference between average people and the top people in most companies.

The top people always do what is expected . . . and then some.

They are thoughtful of others, they are considerate and kind . . . and then some.

They meet their responsibilities fairly and squarely . . . and then some.

They can be counted on in an emergency . . . and then some.

I am thankful for people like this, for they make the world a better place.

Their spirit of service is summed up in these three little words . . . and then some."

Based on my own experience in building a publishing company with 54 magazines, I do not believe it is possible for anyone to rise above mediocrity without developing the habit of performing more service and better service than is actually paid for in dollars and cents. The person who makes it a habit to do this is usually regarded as a leader, and without exception, such people will rise to the top in their profession or business, regardless of other handicaps that may stand in their way.

An individual who renders this sort of service is also sure to attract the attention of people who will start a lively competition for his or her services. No one ever heard of competition over the services of the person who performs as little work as possible to get by or someone who does their work in a careless manner or with an unwilling spirit.

All of the ability on earth, all of the knowledge recorded down the ages, all of the education in the world, will not create a profitable market for the services of a man or woman who renders as little service as possible and makes the quality as poor as will pass. On the other hand, the spirit of willingly performing more work and better work than one is paid to perform is sure to bring its just reward.

In all the time that I have known him, my mentor Joe has modelled this philosophy of doing more and giving more and it is something that I have tried to pass along to my own daughters and all of the staff at Canada Wide Media as we strive to go above and beyond for the customers who have made us a success.

"If you are given a chance to be a role model, I think you should always take it because you can influence a person's life in a positive light, and that's what I want to do. That's what it's all about."
— Tiger Woods

47

ELIMINATE THE UN-WOW

---

*"We first make our habits and then
our habits make us."*
— John Dryden

I've noticed in recent years that in our culture we use the expression "Wow!" a lot, whether it is to describe an exhilarating experience, a book that really impressed us or a new restaurant that we couldn't stop talking about, we like to share our "wow" experiences with others. But there are also other less desirable things that sneak into our lives that my friend and fellow Speakers Roundtable member Nido Qubein likes to call the "un-wows."

The un-wows are the various things we take for granted and let slip when we get lazy or complacent about our day-to-day routine — and although we inadvertently share them with our friends, family, co-workers and customers, I'm sure they wish we wouldn't.

Whether it is the way we always show up a few minutes late for appointments, the fact that we don't respond to emails in a timely manner or how we try to multi-task while serving customers rather than giving our undivided attention, the un-wows are the little things that add up and show the people around us that we don't really care what they think or whether we are meeting their needs.

If you want to Soar Higher in your life, you need to discover as many of your un-wows as you can and then just get rid of them. If you don't know what your un-wows are, don't be afraid to ask the people around you for a little assistance. Nido describes an un-wow as anything that is an irritant to your customer (it also applies to your employees, friends, spouse, etc.).

Nido identified several un-wows in his organization when he became president of High Point University (a small, prestigious school located in High Point, North Carolina) and here's how he and his team dealt with each of them:

- Students no longer pay for on-campus parking. It's free. As Nido explains, "Other schools do it, but paid parking is ridiculous. We're already charging them for the education."
- All laundry services are free. "It's an irritant for students to have to carry quarters and detergent."
- Benches, hammocks and landscape sculptures were added throughout the campus. "We want to create beautiful student destination spots, so they have reasons to mingle."
- The cafeteria was overhauled and a new chef was hired. In addition, an orchestra plays during lunch. "Students used to come in, eat bad food, slam it down and leave. It was a lousy experience."
- Professors now eat in the cafeteria, at the same tables with students. "We want full access to our teachers and a sense of camaraderie between students and faculty."
- The financial part of Admissions used to be in a different building from Financial Aid. The two were combined in one location and called Financial Planning. "It's rude to make busy

parents drive across campus just to get their kid enrolled."
- Decorative brick pathways have been constructed where students were short-cutting across grass. "It's the math teacher's fault anyway. He teaches them the shortest distance between two points is a straight line. Basically, our customers were telling us where the sidewalks should have been."

Why did Nido think that these changes were important to his organization? Because, as he explains, "You can't teach the value of joy, work and community. They must be demonstrated. It's the leader's job to inform, inspire and entertain."

What un-wows could you eliminate from your organization and from your own personal habits?

48

THE DIRECTOR OF FIRST IMPRESSIONS

The receptionist/switchboard operator at my company has a new nameplate at her desk. The nameplate reads, "Director of First Impressions." The decision to provide her with an official title came with the realization of just how important her job is to the success of everyone at Canada Wide Media Limited.

"How so?" you might ask.

For many years, perhaps like most companies, we viewed this job as a low entry position and we assumed a quick week of training was sufficient. We were wrong. We thought this position was simply about answering the phone and putting calls through to the various departments. Then it dawned on us, the receptionist/switchboard operator is the very first point of contact with our company and the efficiency, attention to detail and pleasantness he or she displays to our customers makes all the difference in the world.

So we searched around for a mature, experienced switchboard operator and we gave her the title Director of First Impressions. Maria wanted the job, she wanted to be here and she made such an impression on us that we renamed the position for her. Having the sign on her desk has two purposes: people coming in off the street see that sign and they know the person who sits behind the front desk is both a professional and a valued part of the Canada Wide team. In addition, Maria herself sees it every morning when she comes in and understands how important her job is and so she takes her responsibility very seriously, treating everyone with courtesy, respect and doing the utmost to provide the service they require.

No matter what business you are in, you can't disregard the importance of your receptionist/switchboard operator, because he or she is the first line of contact with everyone you do business with. Some people will hire a guard-dog type of person to man the front desk and in my mind it is a big mistake. For my money, I want someone who is pleasant, helpful and efficient, someone just like Maria.

If you're still skeptical, think about the last time that you went to meet someone at their office or showed up for an appointment. When you walked in the door, who was the first person you met? Most likely it was the receptionist sitting at the front desk. What do you remember about that encounter, was the person attentive, welcoming and helpful or distracted, dismissive and unaccommodating? Now think about how that first impression affected the way the rest of your visit went and how it influenced your interest in doing business with that company.

As my mentor Mel Cooper would often say, "If you serve customers with creativity, competence and commitment, the competition may catch on, but they will never catch up." Because we've let her know how important she is to our company and given her the authority to do her job, Maria makes sure that she does her very best to take care of every person who walks through the door, whether it is a prospective new client, a nervous intern showing up for their first day of work or a courier delivering a package. Her name is Maria Vlasenko and you can call her at 604-299-7311 and hear for yourself.

By telling your employees how important they are to your success, you empower them to be the ambassadors that you need them to be for your business. It also helps to make their job more interesting and promotes the sense of self-respect that comes from a job well done.

Help others to help you by publicly acknowledging their contribution to your success.

49

GOOD OLD-FASHIONED PRIDE

I recall a story that billionaire Jimmy Pattison told me one time about how he had an annual pride convention for his many employees where upon opening the first meeting of the day, he proceeded to pair people up. Once everyone had a partner, he gave them a mop and a pail and assigned them to clean each other's rooms.

When everyone was done, Jimmy had the hotel staff inspect each room and grade it based on their professional opinion. The purpose of the exercise was to help his employees learn the importance of service and humility in business and to send home the message that no one in the organization is above any task.

As Robin Sharma writes in his book, *The Greatness Guide*, "There is no such thing as an unimportant day. Each one of us is called to greatness. Each one of us has an exquisite power within us. Each one of us can have a significant impact on the world around us — if we so choose. But for this power that resides internally to grow, we need to use it."

The point here is that we should take pride in everything we do and be willing to do any job that we would expect others to do. As a leader, nothing should be beneath you. Leadership begins in the trenches, so set the example that you want others to follow. As General George S. Patton is famous for saying, "Give direction, not directions."

Here are some suggestions to help you build pride in your business:

- Provide sufficient training for all new employees, new tasks and new programs
- Set realistic deadlines
- Share information and encourage feedback
- Offer recognition for a job well done
- Allocate sufficient resources to accomplish goals
- Develop clear standards and measure outcomes
- Offer coaching and give employees the authority to make decisions
- Reward performance in a tangible manner (through incentives and promotions)

"One of the great undiscovered joys
of life comes from doing everything one
attempts to the best of one's ability.
There is a special sense of satisfaction, a
pride in surveying such a work, a work
which is rounded, full, exact,
complete in its parts, which the superficial
person who leaves his or her work in
a slovenly, slipshod, half-finished condition,
can never know. It is this conscientious
completeness which turns any work into art.
The smallest task, well done, becomes
a miracle of achievement."
— Og Mandino

50

WHAT ARE YOU DOING FOR FREE?

Whenever we are in Palm Springs, my wife and I like to visit one of our favourite restaurants, LG's Steakhouse, which is owned and operated by Leon and Gail Greenberg. As Leon is fond of saying, LG's is locally owned and nationally known. He's not kidding. The restaurant has been in *Tom Horan's Top Ten Steakhouses Hall of Fame* for more than three years. It has also received the *Wine Spectator* Award of Excellence and the *Zagat Survey*'s rating of "Best Steak in Town."

Located just minutes from Palm Springs in the town of Palm Desert, California, part of LG's charm comes from being housed in the oldest adobe building in town. Adding to its charm is the impressive 12-foot double doors carved from Saguaro cactus that provide entrance to the restaurant. After receiving a personal tour of the entire operation, I can say without a doubt that they take their steak very seriously here. So seriously, in fact, that they dry-age their prime beef on premises, something that no other restaurant within 100 miles can claim. If you're not a steak aficionado, dry-aging enhances and intensifies the distinctive flavour and tenderness associated with prime steaks. It is a time-consuming and costly method, but for LG's it is just one of the special touches that sets their restaurant above the competition.

Another special touch is the fact that LG's is one of the few remaining restaurants that make a special Caesar salad right at you table. No premixed Caesar dressing from them. They start from scratch every time and prepare a perfect dressing right before your eyes. In addition, every customer they serve receives the Caesar salad recipe printed out on quality paper that they can take away with them for free. They have been doing this for 16 years.

Retired U.S. General Colin Powell once said, "Success is the result of perfection, hard work, learning from failure, loyalty and persistence."

LG's Steakhouse is living proof that this "formula for success" really does work. With their permission, I have included the recipe for their Caesar salad dressing on the following page. I hope you will enjoy it as much as Kay and I do.

While you're whipping up a batch of dressing, ask yourself this: "What am I doing for 'free' to add to my success?" and "What more can I do to set myself above the competition?"

Classic Caesar Salad
Serves 2

10 oz. Romaine lettuce, chopped in 1-inch squares
1 oz. anchovies (approximately 2)
1 Tbsp. fresh garlic, pressed
1 Tbsp. Dijon mustard
1/2 Tbsp. Worcestershire sauce
1 egg yolk, coddled
1/2 cup good-quality virgin olive oil
1 Tbsp. lemon juice
2 Tbsp. red wine vinegar
1/4 cup parmesan cheese, freshly grated
1 cup seasoned croutons, homemade preferred
Freshly ground black pepper

Place anchovies and fresh garlic in a wooden salad bowl. Crush into a fine paste with two dinner forks. Add Dijon mustard and Worcestershire sauce to the paste and stir. Add egg yolk and continue to stir. *Slowly* add olive oil while continuously stirring. Add lemon juice, red wine vinegar and half of the parmesan cheese. Stir. Place Romaine lettuce in dressing mixture and toss, making sure to coat all sides of the lettuce leaves. Add croutons and remaining parmesan cheese. Toss lightly. Serve on cold plates with chilled forks. Sprinkle with ground pepper to taste.

Bon appétit!

51

WHAT WOULD DONALD TRUMP DO?

A speaking associate of mine, Harvey McKay, who is with the National Speakers Association, has often said that it's the people you *don't* fire who cause you the biggest problems — not the ones whom you do.

Vancouver business executive Jake Kerr agrees and notes that it is an issue for many business owners. Kerr held a retreat at a resort in Whistler, B.C., with 10 similar-minded Vancouver business leaders. One of the projects they undertook during the retreat was to each take time alone to make a list of five elements that they believed they could have done better to be even more successful in business.

When they returned to share their five points, the group found that while they had a wide cross-section of other concerns, the common element that each of the five shared was, "I wish I had fired certain people earlier."

They're not alone. A majority of business owners admit they're scared to fire employees — even the incompetent ones or those who, through their obnoxious behaviour and constant bullying, often cause good employees to quit. This is despite the fact that human resources studies show one of the biggest costs in both time and money to organizations is the management of poor performance (i.e., keeping employees who are a drag on productivity).

How do you find the courage to say, "You're fired!"? Let's face it, we're not all Donald Trumps. In a national survey conducted in the United States, 61 per cent of small-business owners said they find it hard to fire an employee no matter how bad they are. But firing an employee shouldn't be an emotional decision. Instead, it should be a decision that is taken based on a documented record of poor performance. In addition to doing regular performance reviews with employees and keeping detailed records, no matter how small, companies also need to have a formal termination process in place to aid them in dismissing employees who do not meet expectations.

Here are three more important reasons why you should act quickly to get rid of the bad apples in your company:
- Toxic people damage your organization.
- The longer you allow them to stay, the more damage they do.
- When you don't do anything about bad employees, people begin to doubt your leadership.

Following are some do's and don'ts from experts on how to handle firing an employee.

Do:
- Get right to the point. Avoid a long build-up to soften the blow as it will only confuse the point.
- Detail clearly why the employee is being terminated and the effective date of the termination.
- Focus your discussion on performance-related issues.
- Let your employee respond if they have something to say in response.
- If possible, offer the employee an opportunity to resign.
- Inform the employee of any rights or entitlements that they may have coming.
- Ensure the return of any property that belongs to the company.

- Cover all areas of security, including computer passwords and access to company property or data.
- Arrange for the employee to remove personal effects in private.
- End on a positive note. Thank the employee for their contributions and wish them luck in the future.
- Document the termination conference.

Don't:

- Don't give an employee false hope and say you'll help them to find a new job.
- Don't say, "I feel really bad about this." Saying these things only makes the situation worse.
- Don't get defensive or pass the buck and say the firing was not your idea.
- Don't interrupt, contradict or try to defend yourself or the company. Arguing will only create resentment and frustration on the part of the employee.
- Don't assess blame or make apologies, but simply explain that the company's needs don't match the employee's particular skills.
- Don't debate with the employee. Give honest answers, but don't debate.
- Don't use words like "incompetent" or "dishonest." Focus on performance.
- Don't discuss the termination with anyone other than the employee and those directly involved.

It's the people you <u>don't</u> fire
who cause you the biggest problems
— not the ones whom you do.

BUILDING
RELATIONSHIPS

52

LIFT UP THE ONES YOU LOVE

"If you want to lift yourself up,
lift up someone else."
— Booker T. Washington

Early in my career I did a lot of gigs as a stand-up comedian. At that time, wife jokes were standard fare on the comedy circuit and so invariably, I would tell jokes about my wife in my routine. For the most part, they were the kind of one-liners that often make the rounds as "dumb blonde" jokes aimed at getting a cheap laugh. For example, "I told my wife I was going to have an affair and she asked me who would be doing the catering."

Kay never said anything to me about the content of my routine and I didn't really think anything of the jokes or relate it to the relationship that I have with my wife until one day when I was asked to entertain at a Young Life retreat. Following my performance, Jack Mortinson, the director of Young Life in Calgary, Alberta, took me aside and told me how offensive these jokes must be to Kay and the effect that they were likely having on her self-esteem. "Whether she says anything or not, you can be sure that she is dying inside every time you speak," he said.

Right then and there, I decided that I would never again make fun of Kay and that whenever I did speak about her in front of an audience, I would always lift her up and talk about how proud I am to be her husband. I am grateful to Jack Mortinson for teaching me an important lesson. It is one that I have carried through more than 30 years of marriage to a wonderful woman.

Remember to lift up the people you love.

Talking about them in a demeaning or derogatory way is a form of abuse like any other and over time it will eat away at your relationship.

53

LEADING WITH KINDNESS

As I've mentioned in my previous books, every week I write an "Insight" that is delivered at the end of the day on Friday to the desk of every person who works at Canada Wide Media (so it will be the first thing my staff see on Monday morning). Here's one of the Insights that I shared earlier this year:

A company, feeling that it is time for a shake-up, hires a new CEO. This new boss is determined to rid the company of all slackers. On a tour of the facilities, the CEO notices a guy leaning on a wall. The CEO walks up to the guy and asks, "And how much money do you make a week?"

A little surprised, the young fellow looks at him and replies, "I make $300 a week. Why?"

The CEO then hands the guy $1,200 in cash and screams, "Here's four weeks' pay, now get out and don't come back!"

As the young man makes a beeline for the door, one of the workers, with a sheepish grin on his face, mutters, "You sure made his day. He's the pizza delivery guy from Dominos."

Although we all want to have everyone in the company give their best effort on the job, people are seldom willing or able to when they feel that every move they make is being scrutinized or when the possibility of termination is constantly hanging over their head. Aggressive tactics such as those used by the CEO in the above story cost companies dearly because they don't just scare the slackers who do as little as possible, they also intimidate hardworking, dedicated workers and create an atmosphere of fear and mistrust.

You don't have to be a jerk to be a strong leader and being a kind, compassionate person doesn't make you a wimp.

In their book *Leading With Kindness,* authors William F. Baker and Michael O'Malley, Ph.D., turn the old saying, "nice guys finish last" on its ear and explain how successful leaders are able to accomplish much more with kindness and empathy than they are with aggression. However, Baker and O'Malley stress that it's important not to confuse kindness with "weakness, indulgence or mere likability." Being genuinely kind, they say, is to clearly communicate expectations and goals, push colleagues to improve and excel and mentor employees to take on difficult tasks and challenge their abilities. In listing the hallmarks of successful leaders, the authors include: compassion, integrity, gratitude, authenticity, humility, honour and the importance of maintaining credibility with one's employees and clients.

People will forget what you said. They will forget what you did. But they will never forget how you made them feel. Be kind, learn to listen and be sensitive to the needs and expectations of the people you lead.

"Treat your people well and they
will treat your customers well . . .
help people get to their goals and they'll
happily help you get to yours."
— Robin Sharma

54

BUILD YOUR INFLUENCE

There's an old expression, "It's not what you know, but who you know that matters," and whether we like it or not, it's the truth. It's based on a simple fact; whether you're Bill Gates, the mayor of a small town or the fellow down the street, when you need something done, the first place you turn is to the people you already know. For that reason, if you truly want to open doors and make things happen in your career, you must seek out those who have influence within your community.

How do you get to know the most influential business leaders in your city?

It's easier than you think. You can start by subscribing to your local newspaper and watching the 6 p.m. regional news in your market. You can also subscribe to the best-read regional business magazine — here in B.C., it's *BCBusiness* magazine which was named Magazine of the Year by the Western Magazine Awards Foundation — I know because I just happen to own it.

The next step . . .

Using these resources make a list of the 100 most influential business and political leaders in your town or city then set about getting to know them, and more importantly, make sure they know you and what your company does.

How do you do this?

By joining the organizations they belong to, volunteering with the charities with which they are identified and donating services or money to support their causes. You can also communicate with them directly by sending clippings of interest that could help improve their business. If you write books, make sure that everyone receives a signed copy of your book. If you don't, send them a sample of your product or offer a complimentary service for them to try.

Does it work?

This is a strategy that I have used for years and in my career I have met four Canadian Prime Ministers, the Prime Minister of the United Kingdom, Her Majesty Queen Elizabeth II, a few princes and princesses, dozens upon dozens of millionaires, a few billionaires and just about every provincial and municipal politician in my region of the country.

The best part of all is that if you spend a lifetime doing this, not only will the rewards to you and your business be endless, but at some point you will also become exactly the kind of influential person whom others want to know.

For example, because of my visibility as a public speaker and author, Mark Andrew, a VP with Fairmont Hotels, recently bought 12 copies of my book *The Power of Tact*, along with 12 CDs of the book to take along with him on a trip to Washington, D.C., where he would be calling on potential clients who might be planning to hold their next meeting or convention in Vancouver. As he met with these people to encourage them to book their event at the Fairmont Hotel Vancouver, he gave each of them one of the books or CDs as a thank-you gift.

Likewise, Mayor Wayne Wright of the City of New Westminster in B.C., who went with Premier Gordon Campbell to open the B.C. Pavilion in Beijing for the 2008 Olympic Games, asked me to prepare a dozen packages, each with a copy of my latest book — along with a bookmark in Chinese explaining who I am and what I do — wrapped in gold paper to give to the Chinese dignitaries he would be meeting during his trip.

A word of caution here, influence is very much like respect: it's something that must be earned. Therefore, focus on building relationships and friendships over the long haul. Endeavour to earn the trust and respect of those you admire. When people know you, respect you and trust you, they will gladly help you and do business with you.

So get started today and put yourself in front of the people you want to meet by emceeing as many events as you can, chairing luncheons, organizing dinners or hosting fundraising events. Do this regularly and then you too might become a person of influence for others.

"People will sit up and
take notice of you if you will
sit up and take notice of
what makes them sit up
and take notice."
— Frank Romer

OPPORTUNITY
KNOCKS

55

PINK-SLIP ENTREPRENEURS

For many, the thought of being laid off, fired, given the boot or otherwise "let go" is the most frightening thing in the world. While for others, it is just the kick in the pants they need to embark on the adventure of being an entrepreneur. In my book *The Runway of Life* I tell the story of how those two little dreaded words, "You're fired!" led me to buy a fledgling magazine and start my own publishing company.

Turns out there are plenty of well-known entrepreneurs who got their start the same way I did. Home Depot's Bernie Marcus and Arthur Blank were pink-slip entrepreneurs, so too was David Neeleman of JetBlue Airways and even *Harry Potter* author J.K. Rowling, who lost her job for writing short stories during work hours.

The great part about launching a business today is that with all of the technology we have available to us, you can run a business from just about anywhere. In fact, statistics show that in the U.S. 49 per cent of all companies are now operated from a home office and I'm pretty sure that Canada has a similar ratio.

The other great part about becoming an entrepreneur — and the reason that many people take the plunge — is that you gain control over your life and the direction of your career. That's not to say that it isn't hard work, because it is. Chances are, that in the beginning at least, you will be working longer hours and putting more energy into your business than you have put into anything you have done up until now. The plus side is that when you're doing it for yourself and you love what you do, it's not really work, is it? As Confucius said, "Find work that you love and you will never have to work another day in your life." Another plus is that *you* benefit directly from all your hard work, not your boss or someone else.

Running your own business can also provide you with greater flexibility to meet the needs of your family, something that pays the kind of dividends that can't be calculated in monetary terms. With two of my three daughters now working alongside me at Canada Wide Media Limited, I'm happy to say that being a business owner has provided me with the opportunity to continue to be close to my children as they have grown into successful adults. It's just one more added bonus.

One bit of advice: if you are thinking about becoming an entrepreneur and you don't like the paperwork side of running your own business, like dealing with the administrative and accounting work, it is best to hire a manager early on to take care of these for you while you focus on what you do best, building the business and taking care of your customers.

You don't have to wait for a pink slip to start living the life you want. If you have a good idea and the drive to be successful, there's no time like the present to set off on your own adventure.

56

NEVER HAVE LUNCH ALONE

A woman who had had lunch with both William Gladstone and Benjamin Disraeli at different times remarked, "When I had lunch with Gladstone, I was convinced that he was the most brilliant person in the world, and when I had lunch with Disraeli, I came away convinced that I was the most intelligent person in the world."

Having a one-on-one lunch together (rather than a meeting in the office) is a great way to really get to know someone. In the last month or so, since I haven't been doing a lot of speaking engagements, rather than stay in my office during lunchtimes to catch up on paperwork, I decided to take advantage of the opportunity and make as many lunch dates as possible.

Sitting in front of someone is a great way to build your contacts and build your Rolodex, but more importantly, it's a great way to build relationships. The best way to demonstrate to someone that you want to build a relationship is by showing an interest in their ideas and interests. So use your lunch as an opportunity to find out as much as you can about them. The person who asks the questions is generally in control of the conversation. Ask questions that don't have yes or no answers and make lots of notes. Making notes lets the other person know that you value what they have to say and you want to refer back to it later. Some of the best stories that I share in my speeches and my books have come from having lunch with people who were more than happy to share their wisdom and experiences.

Another benefit of not having lunch alone is that it can also result in business opportunities. Despite the fact that the majority of the conversation is not about business, at almost every lunch I've had over the years, I ended up walking away with some sort of commitment . . . whether it was for a charity I support, for my own company or a speaking engagement.

So remember, the next time you have an empty spot on your calendar, don't just grab a sandwich and sit at your desk, pick up the phone and ask someone to lunch.

Need to brush up on your lunch etiquette? Here are a few tips to keep in mind:

1. Be on time. Although it's just good manners, many people think nothing of showing up late and blaming it on traffic, an important last-minute phone call or other business. Showing up late says that you don't value the other person's time as much as your own. Better to leave the office early and take some reading or work with you to look over while you are waiting.

2. Give your full attention to the person you are dining with. Avoid glancing around the room to scope out who else is there; that makes it look as if you are uninterested and there is nothing worse than having a conversation with someone who is only half there.

3. Turn off your cell phone before you sit down to lunch. It's rude to answer your phone at the table (and trust me, no one in the restaurant wants to hear your conversation). It is also rude to pick up the call and then take it outside, leaving your lunch companion sitting alone as if they've been put on hold.

4. Who picks up the tab? If you did the inviting, you are

responsible for the bill, no matter how well-off your guest is. If you are meeting with someone who is giving you valuable advice, you must also pick up the tab and a personal handwritten follow-up note is also appropriate. If the person you are lunching with has saved you money or helped you make more money, send them a gift or gift certificate to show your appreciation.

The best way to demonstrate to someone that you want to build a relationship is by showing an interest in their ideas and interests.

57

IT NEVER HURTS TO ASK

When my Kay and I were first married, we rented a townhouse and lived for a time in Putney, just outside of London, England. Next door to us lived a fellow named Peter Thierry and his wife Carol. In those days I was an aspiring nightclub comic and as Kay and I got to know our neighbours, we discovered that Peter was an independent television producer and his wife was a host on one of the popular TV chat shows.

With a wife of my own to support and hopes of a family in the future, it was important for me to get my career moving, so I asked Peter if there was any way he would produce a demo film for me if I were to write a 20-minute comedy show. Because I didn't really have any money for such an undertaking, I also asked him if there was a possibility that he would be able to produce it at his studio for free and have his wife Carol be the emcee or host for the show. After some discussion and negotiation, his production company said they would give me one hour of studio time on a Thursday and that he would willingly be the producer for free and Carol would be the host. I just had to write it.

With the important details worked out, the studio date was set for three weeks hence and I managed to find some musicians and friends who would also pitch in to help. When our studio time came up it took us exactly 58 minutes to tape the entire show and I left the studio with my very first demo tape for a TV show.

With demo tape in hand, I contacted about a half dozen producers at BBC, ITV and London Weekend Television and invited them to screen the demo. For the occasion I had rented a screening theatre and arranged for some drinks and sandwiches that I really couldn't afford at all so that I could show them the demo video. My presentation concept was that there really wasn't enough new talent on British television and I named the show, *Don't Ask Us, We're New Here.*

Three weeks following the presentation, I signed a contract with John Ammonds, the senior producer at the BBC who produced the highly successful *Morecambe & Wise Show,* for a nine-week run. During the time that our show was on the air, we ended up with between seven and eight million people watching every week. Not bad for a guy who didn't have any contacts or experience in the TV business prior to moving to Putney.

The point that I would like to make is that it doesn't really matter what it is that you want to accomplish — there is always a way to get it done if you use your natural resources. So even if you don't have any money, chances are that you do have friends, and you do have talent, and you do have ability . . . and you never know what others may be willing to do until you ask them. In my experience, as long as you are honest and genuine with people, they will reciprocate in kind. I've used this concept in almost every aspect of my life and as a result it has contributed to my success in so many ways — and helped to form some of the most wonderful friendships along the way.

It is possible to do marvellous things
on a shoestring and you just never know
what might happen when you
enlist the help of others, so go ahead
— it never hurts to ask.

"The answer is always no, unless you ask."
— Patricia Fripp, CPAE

58

A CHANCE ENCOUNTER WITH STEDMAN

I had just stepped off a plane in Vancouver after coming home from Winnipeg and I was walking up the jet way when my cell phone rang. It was my assistant Dale Clarke calling to ask, "Could you go downtown for 10:30 to meet Stedman?" She went on to explain how Candace Newton, who runs an organization called Unlocking Secrets for Women, had phoned out of the blue. She had Stedman in town for something else and she woke up that morning and thought, "Who do I want Stedman to meet while he is here?" and the answer that popped into her head was, "Peter Legge, of course." So that's how it happened.

Talking on the phone with Dale, I have to admit that I had no idea who Stedman Graham was, so I told her, "No, I have things to do and I need to go to the office." But that wasn't nearly the end of it. She phoned me again in the car a short time later and said, "I've set up a lunch for you and Stedman today," and in the background I could hear my two daughters yelling, "Dad, dad, dad, do you have any idea who this is . . . ? It's Oprah's significant other and you've got to have lunch with him and we want to come."

I'm sure you've guessed by now that I didn't go to my lunch meeting with Stedman alone. Along with my daughters, Samantha and Rebecca, I was duly impressed when halfway through the lunch he started talking about one of his books, *The Nine Steps*, and I discovered that Stedman is quite an author and a speaker. Just then I came up with a brilliant idea and I asked him right there on the spot, "What are you doing on June 25?" and invited him to be the keynote speaker at the annual *BCBusiness* Top 100 Luncheon. Stedman graciously accepted. His speech is called *You Can Make It Happen* and he's the nicest guy you could ever meet.

It's amazing what can come out of these impromptu meetings. A lot of my ideas, contacts and connections have come from the people that I have lunch with. I didn't know when I woke up that morning that I was going to sign someone I had never met to be the keynote speaker at the *BCBusiness* Top 100 — which is considered the premier business luncheon of the year in Vancouver — but it does reinforce two important points that I make elsewhere in this book.

The first point is that you need to build your network and get to know the people in your community. There are a lot of people whom Candace Newton could have chosen to introduce to Stedman Graham. I'm happy that she chose me. The second is never to have lunch alone. I'm thankful to Dale for being persistent and booking the lunch despite the fact that I didn't know who Stedman was. If she hadn't, I would have missed out on a great opportunity.

What chance encounters
have turned into great
opportunities in your life?

Are you taking the time
to make the most
of the opportunities that come
your way every day?

NEVER STOP LEARNING

59

A CURIOUS FELLOW

All my life, I have been very big on questions. No matter where I go or whom I meet I'm always curious . . . so I ask a lot of questions. As the old joke goes, "I'm interested to see what makes you tick, because the noise is driving me crazy." Thankfully, most of the people I meet are more than happy to indulge my curiosity and as a result I have made a lot of new friends and gathered hundreds upon hundreds of interesting stories that I am able to share with others.

Curiosity is an important trait of a genius. I don't think you can find an intellectual giant who is not a curious person. Leonardo da Vinci, Albert Einstein and Thomas Edison were all curious individuals who allowed their curiosity to steer them into uncharted territory that eventually led to inventions that changed the world around them.

How can curiosity help you be more successful in life?

Curiosity keeps the mind active. Curious people continually ask questions and search for new ways of doing things. Not only does this help us to learn, it also provides exercise for the brain. Because the brain is like a muscle, this mental exercise keeps it strong, healthy and happy. As it turns out, my own curious nature is something that has helped to keep me young, or at least it has kept my brain young — this according to the technician who took a scan of my brain following a stroke several years ago. When the technician looked at the picture of my brain he told my wife that it looked like the brain of someone almost 20 years younger. After finding out that I read an average of a book a week, he said that my curiosity and interest in learning would definitely explain the youthful condition of my brain.

Curiosity opens up new possibilities. Being curious leads us to explore and discover new ways of thinking and doing what the average person never considers. As a result, curiosity has been the driving force behind most inventions, discoveries and adventures in the history of mankind. Although you may not discover a new continent or the cure for a serious disease, developing a sense of curiosity may help you to find a new career that fits you to a T; or it could inspire you to learn a new language and get out and explore the world around you, all things that would greatly enhance the quality of your life.

Curiosity helps you recognize opportunity. Curious people are always looking for new ideas and new ways to apply the information they learn, this makes them natural problem solvers — a skill that is in high demand in any profession. By feeding your curiosity you are also building marketable business skills.

Curiosity makes life more exciting. When you are curious and actively seeking out new information and experiences, you never find time to be bored. People who indulge their curiosity will always find something that attracts their attention whether it is being in an unfamiliar place, meeting another person for the first time or trying a new kind of food; curious people turn their entire life into one big adventure.

Tips to Maintain Your Curiosity

Don't be afraid to ask questions as if you were five years old.
If you've ever spent time with a five-year-old, you'll know exactly what I mean by this. At that age children are naturally curious

about everything around them and they haven't yet learned to censor their questions. "What is that?" "How does it work?" "Where did it come from?" "Why is it doing that?" It's like having a little journalist following you around. Although I'm not suggesting that you make a nuisance of yourself, most people are happy to indulge your curiosity if you approach them in the right way. The five W's and an H: who, what, where, when, why and how are the stock in trade of the curious person.

Don't let your mind clank shut.
As we grow up and settle into the routines of being an adult, it's easy to narrow our focus and pay less attention to what's happening in the world around us. Unfortunately, when we get stuck in our ways and don't allow new ideas in, our minds start to rust and become less effective. Keeping an open mind and not being afraid to change with the times can help keep the rust at bay. As can a willingness to unlearn those things that no longer make sense and replace them with new ideas that allow you to continue growing and contributing.

Approach learning as an adventure.
Learning shouldn't be a chore. After all, it is the most natural thing that we do from the time we are born. How do children learn best? By approaching it as play. Take a cue from the little ones and allow learning to be fun by following your own sense of curiosity about the world.

Read more about the things that capture your interest.
Reading is a great way to learn and it's something that most people don't do enough. So rather than sitting down to watch television in the evening, why not visit the library or your local bookstore and browse the shelves to find books on topics that

interest you? I particularly enjoy reading biographies of people I admire and I like to keep several books on hand at all times so that I can read whenever I have a few extra moments. Commit to reading one book a week — you, and your life, will change as a result.

Curiosity has been the driving force behind most inventions, discoveries and adventures in the history of mankind.

60

WHO ARE YOUR FIVE?

I find all of those cell-phone advertisements for "my five" ironic because they touch on an important concept that I've mentioned in some of my earlier books. It's the idea that the five people you spend the most time with will have such a profound effect on you that they will even influence how much income you earn.

If you don't believe me, take a look at the five people you spend the most time with. Approximately how much does each person earn? Now work out the average. Chances are very good that your earnings are close to that average.

"Why is that?" you ask.

You've heard it said that if you hang around with criminals, eventually you'll become a criminal or if you hang around with angry, depressed or whining people, you will become one of them. Well, the same is true if you choose to spend your time with positive, happy, optimistic people — you will eventually become one yourself. And if you spend most of your time around motivated, successful, entrepreneurial types, that's what you'll be.

With so much riding on the influences that you choose to let into your life, it's important to surround yourself with people that you admire and want to emulate. Therefore, if you're not happy with the life you have, the best thing you can do for yourself is to look for people who are living the life you want and allow their habits to influence your behaviour.

If you don't know where to start, think about the most positive, encouraging people you know and seek them out. Make a choice to spend time with people who are in a place of happiness and success, and who have strong self-esteem. Those are the people you'll learn the most from, and chances are, they'll be eager to lend a hand (people genuinely love to be asked for help; it's part of human nature).

Another take on "Your Five" is forming a "Mastermind Group" as introduced in Napoleon Hill's book *Think & Grow Rich*. A mastermind group brings together several likeminded people to help and inspire each other. Once a group is formed, members meet regularly to brainstorm ideas, provide objective feedback for each other, create accountability measures to maintain focus, provide support and act as a catalyst for growth, all in an environment of confidentiality, respect and honesty. Through the group synergy, each member gains insights and practical knowledge that can help to improve both their business and personal life.

Having a mastermind group provides you with:
- Positive motivation to work towards your goals
- The perspective of others (getting other valuable points of view)
- An accountability system to propel you higher than you could go on your own
- A valuable support network
- The experience of others (you can learn from someone else's mistakes)
- Encouragement to overcome your fears, especially the fear of change
- Focus
- Forward momentum

• A specific time dedicated to working on your business

Whether you choose to build an informal network with "your five" or a more formal "mastermind group," it's time to get to work on building the life you want. As Henry David Thoreau said, "I know of no more encouraging fact than the unquestionable ability of a human being to elevate their life by conscious endeavour."

You've heard the saying "You are what you eat"? The same goes for your thoughts. Whatever you feed your mind, you will ultimately become.

61

FIND A NEW STRATEGY

One day, there was a blind man sitting on the steps of a building with a hat by his feet and a sign that read, "I am blind, please help." A creative publicist walking by stopped to observe — in doing so, he noticed that the blind man only had a few coins in his hat, so the fellow dropped a few more coins into the hat and without asking for permission, took the sign, turned it around and wrote another announcement. He placed the sign back by the blind man's feet and walked on.

Later that afternoon on his return journey, the publicist walked by the blind man once again and noticed that his hat was now full of both paper money and coins. The blind man recognized his footsteps and asked if it was him who had re-written the sign. He also wanted to know what had been written on it. The publicist responded matter of factly, "It is nothing that is not true, I simply rewrote your message." Then he smiled and went on his way. The blind man never knew it, but his new sign read, "Today is spring and I cannot see it."

It's amazing how just a small adjustment in our strategy can make such a big difference in the results we get. Like the blind man, many times we simply can't see when the strategy we're using isn't working for us. But if you're not getting the results you want, chances are, it's time to try something different. Like the publicist, we need to be creative, resourceful and inventive to Soar Higher.

When you're feeling stuck, actively seek
out new ideas, new opportunities, new
sources of energy and new resources to help
you get back on top of your game.

62

WHEN IN OXFORD

I've heard it said that reading good books is as healthful for the mind as exercise and good nutrition are for the body. Mental protein is found in books that stimulate, inspire, educate, motivate and can change your thinking and ultimately your life.

For over 21 years, I have disciplined myself to read a book a week. That's over 1,000 books to date. When I travel, looking for unusual bookstores is a passionate hobby and something that I never tire of. However, there was one particular book on my list that eluded me for many years. That book is titled, *Man's Search for Meaning* and it was written by Viktor Frankl, an Austrian psychologist who was imprisoned in a concentration camp during the Second World War.

Try as I would on my many trips, I couldn't find a copy anywhere until one summer, while holidaying in England with my wife Kay and our three girls, Samantha, Rebecca and Amanda, we took a day trip to visit Oxford. It was a glorious English day and we decided that there could be no better way to see the city and the famed university than from atop an open-air double-decker bus complete with tour guide.

With these bus tours, there are different spots where you hop off the bus at a particular tourist stop and then hop back on another bus and continue the tour. At one such pick-up spot on Broad Street, we looked down into the street and noticed a place called Blackwell's Book Shop. As we listened, our tour conductor gave us the background: "Benjamin Blackwell founded this store in 1879 and one of the rare aspects of this bookstore is that it is also a tourist attraction, holding 250,000 volumes in what is the largest single room devoted to book sales in Europe, 10,0000 square feet." He went on to say that virtually any book can be bought at Blackwell's.

That was enough motivation to get me out of my seat. I quickly said to my wife and children, "Let's hop off and see if they have Viktor Frankl's book." I don't think I could have been more excited if I were a five-year-old in a 10,000-square-foot candy shop when I stepped into Blackwell's and discovered that they had not only one copy of the book, but five — I bought them all and I couldn't wait to get back to the hotel and start reading. I think it was fitting that I should finally find *Man's Search for Meaning* in Oxford, a city that is dedicated to learning.

In the book, Frankl wrote the following about his experience as a concentration camp prisoner, "Everything can be taken from a man but one thing, the last of human freedoms, to choose one's attitude to a given set of circumstances, to choose one's way."

How powerful, to be responsible for every aspect of our life, no matter what.

As one of my Speakers Roundtable colleagues, Charlie "Tremendous" Jones, famously once said,

"You will be the same person that you are today in five years except for the people you meet, the places you go and the books you read."

Sound advice.

What books have inspired you
to Soar Higher in your life?

Do you make time to read
and expand your knowledge
on a regular basis?

63

WEIRD THINGS
YOU WOULD NEVER KNOW

A shrimp's heart is in its head.

The "sixth sick sheik's sixth sheep's sick" is said to be the toughest tongue twister in the English language.

Rats multiply so quickly that in 18 months, two rats could have over a million descendants.

Wearing headphones for just an hour will increase the bacteria in your ear by 700 times.

If the government has no knowledge of aliens, then why does Title 14, Section 1211 of the Code of Federal Regulations, implemented on July 16, 1969, make it illegal for U.S. citizens to have any contact with extraterrestrials or their vehicles?

In every episode of *Seinfeld* there is a Superman somewhere.

A duck's quack doesn't echo, and no one knows why.

Most lipstick contains fish scales.

Like fingerprints, everyone's tongue print is different.

If you sneeze too hard, you can fracture a rib. If you try to suppress a sneeze, you can rupture a blood vessel in your head or neck and die.

If you keep your eyes open by force, they can pop out.

In a study of 200,000 ostriches over a period of 80 years, no one reported a single case where an ostrich buried its head in the sand.

It is physically impossible for pigs to look up into the sky.

A pregnant goldfish is called a twit.

More than 50 per cent of the people in the world have never made or received a telephone call.

Horses can't vomit.

Butterflies taste with their feet.

In 10 minutes, a hurricane releases more energy than all of the world's nuclear weapons combined.

On average, 100 people choke to death on ballpoint pens every year.

On average people fear spiders more than they do death.

Ninety per cent of New York City cabbies are recently arrived immigrants.

Thirty five per cent of the people who use personal ads for dating are already married.

Elephants are the only animals that can't jump.

Only one person in two billion will live to be 116 or older.

It's possible to lead a cow upstairs . . . but not downstairs.

Women blink nearly twice as much as men.

It's physically impossible for you to lick your elbow.

The Main Library at Indiana University sinks over an inch every year because when it was built, the engineers failed to take into account the weight of all the books that would occupy the building.

A snail can sleep for three years.

No word in the English language rhymes with "month."

Our eyes are always the same size from birth, but our nose and ears never stop growing.

The electric chair was invented by a dentist.

All polar bears are left-handed.

In ancient Egypt, priests plucked *every* hair from their bodies, including their eyebrows and eyelashes.

An ostrich's eye is bigger than its brain.

TYPEWRITER is the longest word that can be made using the letters only on one row of the keyboard.

"Go," is the shortest complete sentence in the English language.

If Barbie were life-size, her measurements would be 39-23-33. She would stand seven feet, two inches tall.

A crocodile cannot stick its tongue out.

The cigarette lighter was invented before the match.

Americans on average eat 18 acres of pizza every day.

. . . And almost everyone
who reads this will try
to lick their elbow.

LIVING WITH GRATITUDE

64

LOOK FOR THE "WOW" IN NOW

Not long ago, I accepted nine speaking gigs in 12 days. All but one of the gigs was in Western Canada, with the very last engagement booked for Seattle, Washington. For those of you who aren't familiar with the industry, many speakers in Canada don't speak nine times a year; I was going to be doing it in 12 days.

The second-to-last gig on my schedule was to be in the town of Taber, Alberta, and by the time my plane touched down in Calgary I was beating myself up, telling myself that I must be crazy for thinking I could do this.

I was picked up at the Calgary airport at noon and driven to Taber, which is about three hours away, for a presentation with 300 people and then driven back to a hotel in Calgary. I arrived at the hotel at 12:30 in the morning, completely exhausted yet knowing that I'd have to get up in the morning, fly to Vancouver, drive to Seattle and do my last presentation.

I tossed and turned all night, nervous about missing my plane. So when my wake-up call came in the morning, I was overtired, negative and grumpy. Arriving at the airport, I went to the check-in, got my boarding pass and then headed to Starbucks where I picked up a much-needed cup of coffee before heading to my departure gate. I got on the plane and found my seat in business class, then sat there thinking about how much I was dreading the flight.

Just then, a blonde 11-year-old girl in pigtails stepped onto the plane. From the look of excitement on her face, it was clear that she had never been on a jet before. As she stood there looking down the long row with so many seats on each side, she turned to her mother and said, "Wow, mommy, this is amazing!"

At that moment, seeing her reaction to something that I had been taking for granted, it hit me, "Wow indeed!" I was flying business class with my Starbucks coffee and when I arrived in Vancouver I was going to get in my Jaguar and drive down to Seattle where I would be paid to speak to a group of people — something that I absolutely love to do — and then I would return to Vancouver and spend a relaxing weekend with the love of my life. Could life get any better than that? I don't think so.

As I sat there through the remainder of the flight, I looked around me with a renewed sense of appreciation and thought about all of the "wow" things that I enjoy in my life every day and how lucky I really am.

What are some of the "wow" things in your life that you take for granted?

Take time to appreciate what you have and all that you have accomplished. If you need something to remind you from time to time, make a list and put it somewhere visible.

"Either everything is a miracle,
or nothing is a miracle."
— Albert Einstein

65

DON'T FORGET TO RETURN THE FAVOUR

In the late '60s, the legendary comedian and singer Rolf Harris got his start performing at Ken Stauffer's famous The Cave Supper Club on Howe Street in Vancouver. Rolf and I shared the same talent agent, Phyllis Rounce, when I had worked as a comedian on the club circuit in England.

Back in 1969, during a tour of Australia's Arnhem Land with his family, Rolf briefly stayed with a man named Ted Egan. Ted sang him the song below, which Rolf recorded on tape. Back in England, Rolf persuaded his television producer to use the song, but then discovered he had lost the tape. Rolf had to telephone Ted some 12,000 miles away in Canberra and have him perform the song over the phone. Alan Braden arranged the song for the TV show and the audience loved it so much that Rolf decided to record it. As a result, the song was at the top of the Hit Parade for seven weeks over Christmas 1969. Here are the lyrics:

Two Little Boys
(Morse — Madden arr. Braden) H. Darewski Music / EMI / Redwood Music (P) 1969; Cond. Alan Braden; Produced by Mickey Clarke

Two little boys had two little toys
Each had a wooden horse
Gaily they played each summer's day

Warriors both of course
One little chap then had a mishap
Broke off his horse's head
Wept for his toy then cried with joy
As his young playmate said

Did you think I would leave you crying
When there's room on my horse for two
Climb up here Jack and don't be crying
I can go just as fast with two
When we grow up we'll both be soldiers
And our horses will not be toys
And I wonder if we'll remember
When we were two little boys

Long years had passed, war came so fast
Bravely they marched away
Cannon roared loud, and in the mad crowd
Wounded and dying lay
Up goes a shout, a horse dashes out
Out from the ranks so blue
Gallops away to where Joe lay
Then came a voice he knew

Did you think I would leave you dying
When there's room on my horse for two
Climb up here Joe, we'll soon be flying
I can go just as fast with two
Did you say Joe I'm all a-tremble
Perhaps it's the battle's noise
But I think it's that I remember
When we were two little boys

Do you think I would leave you dying
There's room on my horse for two
Climb up here Joe, we'll soon by flying
Back to the ranks so blue
Can you feel Joe I'm all a-tremble
Perhaps it's the battle's noise
But I think it's that I remember
When we were two little boys

Whenever I recall the words to this song, I can't help but think of myself and Ray Addington. As you'll know if you've read my other books, Ray is one of my three mentors and someone who has been generous with his support, guidance and encouragement throughout the years. When I won the Marketing Executive of the Year award in 1991 from the Sales and Marketing Executives, as a special surprise, Ray presented me with a letter of congratulations from none other than the former Prime Minister of Britain, Margaret Thatcher. Having been born in England and also being a big fan of Maggie Thatcher, I was over the moon at receiving this thoughtful gift.

Seventeen years later, I received a call from the Fraser Institute where Ray had been chair for 20 years, informing me that they were hosting a special evening to honour Ray upon his retirement from the board. They asked if I would consider speaking at the event or being the emcee. Knowing that this was an important milestone for Ray and remembering what he had done for me in 1991, a quote from Scottish theologian William Barkley came to mind as I pondered how I could make this occasion special and memorable. Barkley said, "Always give without remembering; always receive without forgetting."

Knowing that Ray was as big a fan of Maggie Thatcher as I am, I wondered if I could do the same for him as he had done for me. I decided that it was certainly worth a try so I got in touch with Maggie Thatcher and sent her a copy of the letter she had written for me along with as much material as I could find on the Fraser Institute and asked her if she would do a letter for Ray. Following a few phone calls, several emails and some letters back and forth, the letter arrived the morning of the dinner and during the event it was read aloud to the audience. Not only did it blow everyone away, but Ray was absolutely thrilled and I was happy to do for him exactly what he had done for me, just like the two boys in the song.

Think of the people in your life
who have given to you without expecting
anything in return. Perhaps it's time
to return the favour.

What can you do for them to
acknowledge that debt?

66

BLAH, BLAH, BLAH

One of the many joys that come from seeing your children grow into wonderful, capable adults is that at some point they too become parents and your life takes on yet another wonderful dimension as a grandparent.

As someone who is thoroughly enjoying her new role, my wife Kay is thrilled to have our young grandson Benjamin each week on Tuesdays and Wednesdays. I don't get to spend nearly as much time with Benjamin, but we are fortunate to occasionally take family holidays where everyone comes along. On one such vacation last Christmas, I told young Benjamin that I was going to teach him some media speech so I sat him down beside me and said, "Benjamin, repeat after me: blah, blah, blah."

Recognizing that he comes by the gift of the gab honestly, Benjamin naturally caught on right away and for the rest of the holiday, whenever a family member asked him to give his "speech" he immediately responded with, "Blah, blah, blah."

When the vacation was over, I returned to my busy work schedule where speaking engagements can frequently take me away from home for weeks at a stretch. As a result, there was a period of time in the early spring where I hadn't seen Benjamin for almost three weeks, so I decided to go home early one Tuesday afternoon to spend some time with him while he was at the house.

When she saw me walk through the front door, Kay turned

to our little grandson and asked, "Do you remember the speech, blah, blah, blah?" Hearing the words I had taught him several months before, his face lit up and he came running toward me shouting, "Granddad, Granddad, blah, blah, blah."

Kay and I couldn't help but laugh out loud as I scooped him up and gave him a big hug.

Having a little grandson to spoil is a real treat for me and watching how quickly he is growing and changing right before my eyes makes me realize just how wonderful it is that my daughters have all remained close by. It reminds me how important it is to take time to make memories with those you love.

I hope you will always remember to do the same.

Don't take a single moment with those you love for granted.

67

THE WHALE

I read a front-page story in one of San Francisco's local newspapers, the *SF Chronicle*, about a female humpback whale that became entangled in a spider web of crab traps and lines. She was weighted down by hundreds of pounds of traps that caused her to struggle to stay afloat. She also had hundreds of yards of line rope wrapped all around her body including her tail and a line tugging in her mouth.

A fisherman spotted her just east of the Farralone Islands (outside the Golden Gate) and radioed an environmental group for help.

Within a few hours, the rescue team arrived and determined that the whale was in such dire straits that the only way to save her was to dive in and untangle her. It was a very dangerous proposition considering that one slap of her tail could kill a rescuer.

The team worked together for hours with curved knives and eventually freed the whale.

When she was free, the divers say she swam in what seemed like joyous circles. She then came back to each and every diver, one at a time, and nudged them gently, as if to say "Thank you for helping me."

Some of the team members said it was the most incredibly beautiful experience of their lives. The guy who cut the rope out of her mouth says her eye was following him the whole time and he will never be the same.

It's important to realize that there are some things we cannot do alone (no matter how strong we are) and we will need the help of others, just as there will be times when others need us to step up and help them.

May you, and all those you love,
be so blessed and fortunate as to be
surrounded by people who will
help you get untangled from the things
that are binding you.

And, may you always know the joy of
giving and receiving gratitude.

68

COUNT YOUR BLESSINGS

If you woke up this morning with more health than illness, you are more blessed than the millions who will not survive this week.

If you have never experienced the danger of battle, the loneliness of imprisonment, the agony of torture or the pangs of starvation, you are ahead of 500 million people in the world.

If you can attend a church meeting without fear of harassment, arrest, torture or death, you are more blessed than three billion people in the world.

If you have food in the refrigerator, clothes on your back, a roof overhead and a place to sleep, you are richer than 75 per cent of this world.

If you have money in the bank, in your wallet, and spare change in a dish someplace, you are among the top eight per cent of the world's wealthy.

If your parents are still alive and still married, you are very rare.

If you hold up your head with a smile on your face and are truly thankful, you are blessed because the majority can, but most do not.

If you can hold someone's hand, hug them or even touch them on the shoulder, you are blessed because you can offer a healing touch.

If you can read this page, you are more blessed than over two billion people in the world who cannot read.

Count your blessings every day.

Whenever I speak to an audience about how much abundance we have in our lives, I always say that we can all come up with at least 15 things to be grateful for. I also point out that, interestingly, when you say out loud all of the things that you're grateful for, the things that aren't exactly perfect in your life seem to pale in comparison.

When you are verbally grateful for the blessings in your life, it changes everything . . . most importantly, it changes your attitude.

Even though we may not see them as blessings at first glance, here are some things that we can all add to our list:

Be thankful that you don't already have everything that you want in your life; otherwise, what would there be to look forward to?

Be thankful for your challenges; they will build your strength and character.

Be thankful when you're tired and weary because it means that you have made an effort.

Be thankful when you don't know something for it gives you the opportunity to learn.

Be thankful for your limitations, as they provide opportunities for improvement.

Be thankful for your mistakes, as they will teach you valuable lessons.

Be thankful for the difficult times for they challenge you to grow.

ABOUT THE AUTHOR

Dr. Peter Legge, O.B.C. • L.L.D. (Hon) • D.Tech. (Hon)
• CSP • CPAE • HoF

Peter Legge is Chairman and CEO of Canada Wide Media Limited, the largest independently owned publishing company in Western Canada, controlling a network of over 50 magazines across the country with over $30 million in sales annually.

In addition, Peter travels the world as a motivational speaker, accepting more than 100 assignments each year from clients who know that when he speaks, his words will be a catalyst for positive change. He has received the prestigious Golden Gavel Award from Toastmasters International and was voted "Top Speaker in North America," in company with Dr. Robert Schuller and Stephen Covey. Peter has also been inducted into the Speakers Hall of Fame by both the National Speakers Association in the United States and the Canadian Association of Professional Speakers.

Peter is tireless in his commitments to many worthwhile organizations. As co-host of the annual Variety — The Children's Charity Telethon for over 33 consecutive years, he has assisted in raising more than $130 million for the charity. He is also an International Ambassador for Variety International.

His efforts have not gone unnoticed. Among his many honours, Peter has received the Golden Heart Award from The Variety Club and has been invested into the Venerable

Order of St. John of Jerusalem, where he has now been promoted to Commander.

He has been awarded the Order of the Red Cross and named Citizen of the Year for his commitment to the community. He has been honoured with an Honorary Doctor of Laws degree from Simon Fraser University, Royal Roads University and the BC Institute of Technology, and he is a past Chair of the Vancouver Board of Trade.

He is the recipient of the Nido Qubein Philanthropy Award presented to him at the NSA Convention in Atlanta in July 2005.

In 2006, he was appointed one of 18 ambassadors to the Vancouver 2010 Olympic and Paralympic Winter Games. In the same year, Sales and Marketing Executives International awarded Peter with the Ambassador of Free Enterprise in Dallas, Texas.

In 2009, Peter was invested into the Order of British Columbia, the highest civilian honour that the province can award.

Peter is also the author of 14 previous books that have inspired thousands of readers the world over with their powerful motivating messages. In all that he has achieved, Peter attributes his success to four factors: persistence, patience, a positive attitude and passion.

To contact Peter Legge, write to:
Peter Legge Management Company Ltd.
4180 Lougheed Highway, 4th Floor
Burnaby, BC V5C 6A7 Canada
Telephone: 604-299-7311
plegge@canadawide.com
www.peterlegge.com

To book Peter Legge to speak at your next convention, AGM or association meeting, contact:

Heidi Christie, manager of Speaker Services,
Peter Legge Management Company Ltd., at 604-473-0332
or *hchristie@canadawide.com*

To order Peter Legge's books, CDs and other products, please contact Heidi Christie at the address above.